RAPA NUI

The Easter Island Legend on Film

RAPA-NUI

The Easter Island Legend on Film

Kevin Reynolds and Tim Rose Price

with Diana Landau

Photographs by Ben Glass
and other contributors

Preface by Kevin Reynolds

A
NEWMARKET
PICTORIAL
MOVIEBOOK

Newmarket Press • New York

Descriptions of the cast, crew, and production are based in part on interviews conducted by Ed Gorsuch, Tig Productions.

Credits and acknowledgments of permissions for illustrations and text from other works are found on page 160.

This book published simultaneously in the United States of America and in Canada.

94 95 96 97 10 9 8 7 6 5 4 3 2 1

Library of Congress Cataloging-in-Publication Data

Reynolds, Kevin, 1952-
Rapa Nui: The Easter Island legend on Film/Kevin Reynolds and Tim Rose Price; photographs by Ben Glass; edited by Diana Landau.
p. cm. — (A Newmarket pictorial moviebook)
ISBN 1-55704-184-9
1. Rapa Nui (Motion picture) 2.Easter Island—History. I. Price, Tim Rose.
II. Landau, Diana, 1950- III. Title. IV. Series.
PN1997.R2373R49 1994
791.43'72—dc20 93-50747
CIP

Quantity Purchases
Companies, professional groups, clubs, and other organizations may qualify for special terms when ordering quantities of this title. For information, write Special Sales, Newmarket Press, 18 East 48th Street, New York, NY 10017, or call (212) 832-3575.

Created by Newmarket Productions, a division of Newmarket Publishing & Communications Company: Esther Margolis, director; Keith Hollaman, editor; Grace Farrell, assistant editor; Joe Gannon, production manager.

Editorial, design, and production services by Walking Stick Press, San Francisco: Diana Landau, editor; Linda Herman, book design; Miriam Lewis, design associate.

Tig Productions staff for *Rapa Nui—The Easter Island Legend on Film*: Kevin Costner, Jim Wilson, Ed Gorsuch, Lynne Whiteford, Allison Conant, Moira McLaughlin, Kathleen McLaughlin, and Magaly Doty.

Manufactured in the United States of America

First Edition

Other Newmarket Pictorial Moviebooks include:

The Age of Innocence: A Portrait of the Film Based on the Novel by Edith Wharton
Bram Stoker's Dracula: The Film and the Legend
City of Joy: The Illustrated Story of the Film
Dances with Wolves: The Illustrated Story of the Epic Film
Far and Away: The Illustrated Story of a Journey from Ireland to America in the 1890s
Gandhi: A Pictorial Biography
The Inner Circle: An Inside View of Soviet Life Under Stalin
Last Action Hero: The Official Moviebook
Neil Simon's Lost in Yonkers

CONTENTS

Preface

A TALE OF WHAT MIGHT HAVE BEEN

by Kevin Reynolds

Easter Island—Rapa Nui—is easily one of the wildest and most haunting places I've ever had the opportunity to visit. Even skeptics would be hard-pressed to deny that there are inexplicable forces at work here... spirits, I suppose.

Whether those forces are what shaped the island's human history, or are the product of that history, is anyone's guess. But the feeling I get, standing amidst the giant *moai* on the slopes of the quarry at Rano Raraku, is that somehow all of this was a painful, obsessive effort to explain what lay over the vast horizon.

Whatever the *moai* makers intended, their obsession led to folly.

Anthropologists and archeologists may scoff at that notion, but if you look at the parallels between what happened on pre-European

Moai *created for the film.*

Crew and extras gathered at the Long Ear village set.

Rapa Nui and what is happening in the modern world, the conclusions are inescapable. All the dark facets of human nature that compel us toward self-destruction were manifested here, in this perfect crucible of isolation.

Rapa Nui—the movie—is not an exact chronicle of what happened on the island. No film could be. It's an extrapolation, a drama of what might have been. I hope that people who see the movie will delve into what *is* known about Rapa Nui—and then they can decide for themselves.

Part One

THE NAVEL OF THE WORLD

Sometime in the distant past, a Polynesian chief named Hotu Matua was forced to flee his homeland, a large, warm, green island called Marae Renga. Most likely he was forced to leave after a defeat in war, although some say that Marae Renga—and all the surrounding lands—sank beneath the sea after a great cataclysm. "One of Hotu Matua's entourage," writes a scholar, "had a prophetic dream of an island to the east with volcanic craters and pleasant beaches, on which six men could be seen. Hotu Matua therefore sent a canoe with six picked men to search for the island and await his arrival there, in order that the [illegible]

Rock carvings (petroglyphs) of bird figures are found all around the Easter Island coastline.

"Days, weeks at sea, at the mercy of the waves, without a glimpse of land. Braving the elements. Kept going through faith in their leader, a group of people—scores of them, men, women and children—were crowded into a catamaran with their animals and plants, their material possessions, and food for a journey of unknown duration. Their navigator stood by the upturned bow of the long vessel and scanned the eastern horizon for tell-tale signs of the 'promised land' which could be their new home...."

After a voyage of six weeks, the legend goes, Hotu Matua and his followers landed at a remote island, which he named Te Pito Te Henua—*literally "land's end" or "end of the world" or "fragment of earth," but often translated as "The Navel of the World."*

More than a millennium later, in 1722, three Dutch ships blundered into this same "fragment of earth" while searching for another South Pacific isle. The first sighting having occurred on Easter Sunday, Captain Jacob Roggeveen rechristened the place Easter Island.

»«

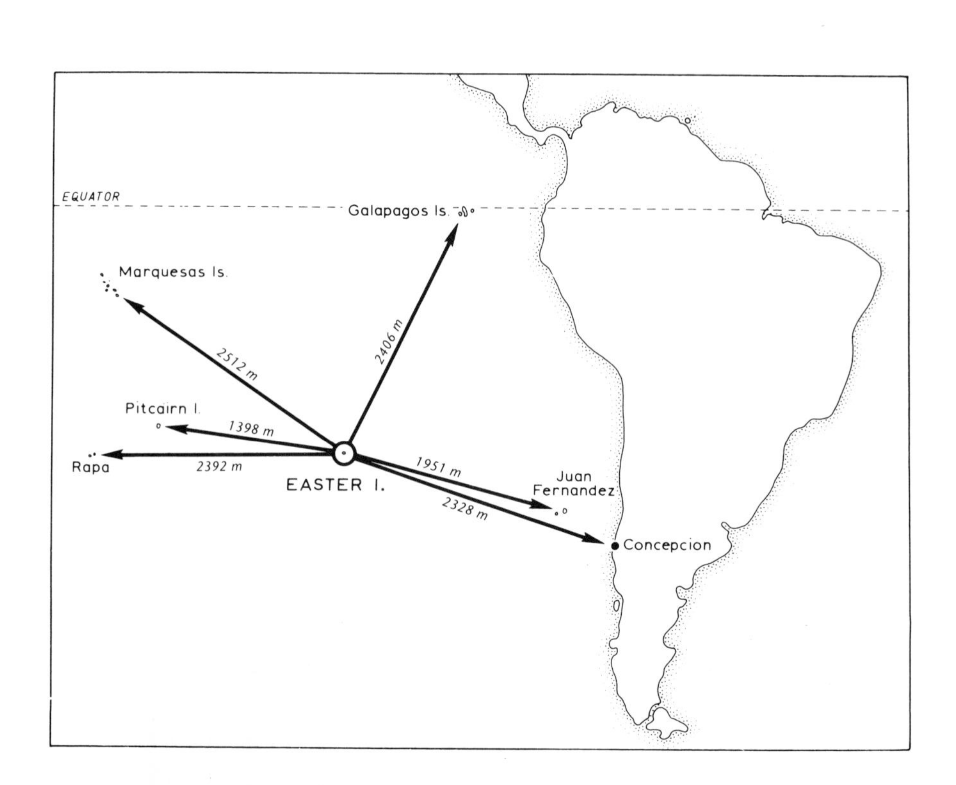

Map showing Easter Island's isolated location in the South Pacific, thousands of miles from any inhabited land.

BUT THE ISLAND has yet another name. About 2,400 miles due west lies a large Polynesian isle called Rapa, which may have been Hotu Matua's homeland. Some nineteenth-century Tahitian sailors believed that Easter Island resembled it, and added the word *nui* ("big") to arrive at the present-day name Rapa Nui.

The early Polynesians were bold sailors, navigating their canoes on long ocean voyages to trade, colonize, or intermarry with families from other islands.

Until a jet airport was constructed in the early 1980s, the only way to reach Easter Island was by sea. And a long hard journey it was: 2,340 miles west from the South American mainland (the port of Concepción in Chile), and 1,400 miles east from its nearest island neighbor, Pitcairn Island, the famed hideout of the *Bounty* mutineers. The Marquesas, the nearest Polynesian archipelago, are almost twice that distance.

Powerful currents and stormy winds in the eastern South Pacific made navigating to Easter Island a tricky proposition even for European ships of the eighteenth and nineteenth centuries. The first to arrive after the Dutch was a Spanish ship in 1770. Four years later the redoubtable English explorer James Cook limped into Easter Island with two ships, seeking respite from circling the globe by a far southern route. He had heard of its existence in Spanish reports, and after weeks sailing the icy

« Concerning the religion of these people, of this we could get no full knowledge because of the shortness of our stay; we merely observed that they set fires before some particularly high erected stone images.... These stone images at first caused us to be struck with astonishment, because we could not comprehend how it was possible that these people, who are devoid of heavy timber for making any machines, as well as strong ropes, nevertheless had been able to erect such images, which were fully 30 feet high and thick in proportion. »

From the journal of Jacob Roggeveen,
Commander of the *Afrikaansche Galei*,
5 April 1722

waters near the Antarctic Circle, any Polynesian port would do.

But what of Hotu Matua and his followers—or whoever did, in fact, first colonize Rapa Nui? Lacking the large ships and sophisticated navigation tools of the Europeans, how did they ever find their way to this atom of land in a vast ocean? And from where did they come? These questions have fascinated visitors and scholars since Roggeveen's crew first set eyes on Rapa Nui and its people, and are still hotly debated.

Whoever they were, they had been surviving on the island since about A.D. 690, according to radiocarbon dating, and perhaps even earlier. They survived apparently by fishing, minimal agriculture, and a little livestock raising (Polynesian voyagers typically loaded their canoes with pigs, fowl, and crop plants). They built reed houses with stone foundations, dug ovens in the earth, and devised enclosures for their stock. By itself none of this would be remarkable; it follows the pattern of Polynesian civilization in many parts of the Pacific.

Facing page: Many of the great statues on Rapa Nui were outfitted with red stone headpieces and staring eyes made of stone and coral. Neither were present when the statues were first found by outsiders, but have been restored on some of the moai.

But the original Easter Islanders took a giant step beyond such basic survival tasks—and in so doing created a mystery that ranks among the greatest of prehistory. They began to carve mammoth icons of their ancestors from volcanic rock quarried in an extinct crater. Not just a few, but literally hundreds of such statues—called *moai*—ranging in size from a few meters to more than 60 feet tall.

They devised a technology to transport these mega-sculptures, weighing tens of tons, several miles across the island, and erect them on altar platforms at the edge of the sea. And they kept on carving them, as if driven by some great compulsion, until their civilization self-destructed (in a rather short span of time, by the evidence). They left scores of half-finished *moai* standing about or lying half-excavated in the quarry, like dinosaurs felled in the aftermath of a earth-shaking catastrophe... and they left their descendants with only dim memories of who they were, why the *moai* were so important, and how it all came apart.

« Apart from his human entourage, perhaps dozens of people, [Hotu Matua's] vessel must have been well supplied with tools, food, and plants and animals. Its two canoes would have been joined by a bridge bearing a mast and a shelter. There would have been a supply of drinking water, to be replenished from downpours during the voyage. Provisions would have included fruits, coconuts, vegetables, and also preserved fish.... On the shelter-floor and in the canoes would be the plants to be used for food, together with medicine, clothing, jewelry and vessels. In small cages or simply tied to the bridge were probably pigs and dogs, and certainly some chickens and rats—the latter were considered a delicacy by the elders.»

Paul Bahn and John Flenley
Easter Island, Earth Island

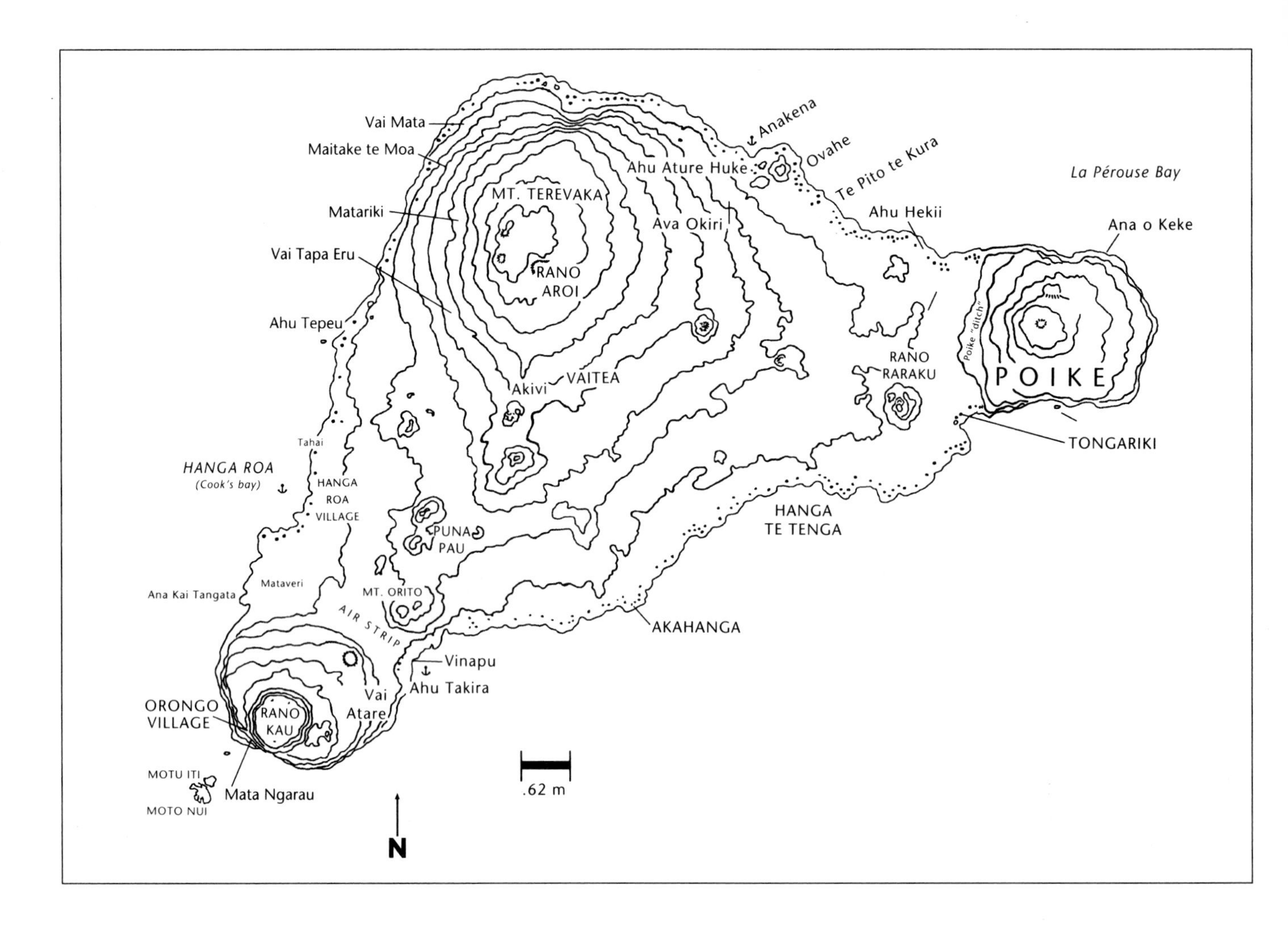

Map of Easter Island, showing elevation contours and major ahu *sites.*

The World Finds Rapa Nui

The existence of Rapa Nui and its astounding artifacts came to light rather late in the great age of discovery, long after both the North and South American continents were colonized, and well after most of the Pacific islands had been mapped and visited. But since that first Dutch ship dropped anchor, it has seized the world's imagination—largely because of the great legacy of its sculpture, unlike any found elsewhere in the world.

Not until this century has that mystery—and others concerning Rapa Nui's prehistoric culture—been seriously investigated. Before that, the rest of the world took note of the enigma but ventured to the island for different purposes, usually involving need or greed.

The earliest European visitors used the island as a very temporary haven from the travails of Pacific voyaging. Members of the Dutch expedition came ashore for only one day. Next to arrive was a Spanish expedition under the command of Felipe González y Haedo, sent in 1770 by the Viceroy of Peru to find and claim the island reported by the Dutch. They lingered at anchor for six days, going ashore several times. Cook's 1774 party rested there for four days; and a French ship

Left: A chief of the Long Ear clan as depicted in the film. Tapa *cloth cloaks, feather headdresses, and elaborately painted ceremonial paddles are emblematic of power throughout Polynesia.*

Below: From an engraving by expedition artist Duché de Vancy depicting the French visit to Rapa Nui in 1786, led by the Comte de la Pérouse. The islander at right is shown surreptitiously making off with a visitor's tricorn hat.

captained by J.F.G. de la Pérouse, arriving in 1786, sent a party on land for just ten hours. Cook himself later wrote that he saw nothing on Rapa Nui "which can induce ships that are not in the utmost distress to touch at this island."

Considering the shortness of their stays, these visitors came away with interesting and useful observations about the place and the people, and some drawings that provide both hints and distortions of island life during that period. All of them remarked on the *moai* phenomenon and marveled that such an apparently backward society could have produced them. The Dutch, based on a cursory inspection, solved the engineering problem to their satisfaction by concluding that the outer shell of the statues was formed with clay and filled with small pebbles, which would be far less heavy than solid rock. Later observers soon corrected that error: one of the Spanish pilots noted in his ship's log, "The material of the statue is very hard stone and therefore weighty; having tried it myself with a hoe it struck fire, a proof of its density."

Some visitors also traded for supplies such as sweet potatoes, bananas, sugar cane, and chickens. The islanders seem to have been generous with their local produce and eager to trade for

Powerful rock paintings and human bones are found in many of Rapa Nui's caves, which were often used as family burial sites. This cave is on the Motu Nui islet. The round-eyed face is probably the creator god Make-Make, who was worshiped on the island late in its prehistory.

hats, cloth, and any metal objects. They were light-fingered thieves, however, and Cook was apparently shortchanged by an enterprising trader who delivered baskets of potatoes containing a top layer of tubers—with rocks underneath.

These infrequent first contacts with Rapa Nui gave rise to other mysteries. The Dutch found an island that seemed to be well-populated (though women were surprisingly scarce) and people who were reasonably well-fed, friendly, and welcoming. By the time the Spanish arrived fifty years later, the population seemed somewhat reduced, or perhaps just more wary of visitors (the Dutch had killed several islanders before departing). Neither of the first two parties mentions seeing any fallen statues.

By the time Cook arrived, only four years later, things had changed dramatically. The English found the islanders in distressingly poor shape: "small, lean, timid and miserable." Their party also saw evidence of agricultural plantations being abandoned and the Rapanui (as the people are often called) using weapons such as clubs and spears. Earlier observers had found them unarmed. Most startling was the discovery that many of the *moai* had been toppled from their platforms, and the ceremonial sites themselves left untended—sometimes with human skeletal remains scattered nearby. What had happened in the intervening years to cause these changes?

The last call by Europeans in the eighteenth century came in 1786, the two French frigates led by La Pérouse—and again, the island had changed face. Instead of the timorous handful of natives encountered by Cook, the French ships were met by some 1,200 islanders. La Pérouse estimated the total population at close to 2,000. Women were as numerous as men, and all seemed in much better physical health than a dozen years earlier. They greeted the visitors warmly (perhaps due to courteous treatment at the hands of Cook's party), and agricultural production was flourishing: "in abundance more than sufficient for the consumption of the inhabitants," according to the ship's doctor.

In the absence of more detailed observations by the explorers, the events that caused such ebb and flow in Rapa Nui's fortunes remain largely unknown. There are some clues, however. All the visitors since Cook noticed that the island contained many caves and rocky hiding places, and speculated that some islanders (women

« We all entered into those caverns in which Mr. Forster and some officers of Captain Cook had first supposed the women might have been concealed. They are subterranean dwelling places....That the inhabitants, however, concealed their women when Captain Cook visited them in 1772 [actually 1774], there can be no doubt; but it is impossible for me to ascertain the cause. It is probable, that to his generous conduct with regard to this people we were indebted for the confidence they showed us, which enabled us to judge more accurately the state of their population....

Instead of meeting with men exhausted by famine...I found, on the contrary, a considerable population, with more beauty and grace than I afterwards met with in any other island; and a soil, which, with very little labour, furnished excellent provisions, and in abundance more than sufficient for the consumption of the inhabitants.... »

French captain J.F.G. de la Pérouse,
on his 1786 visit

When English explorer James Cook visited Rapa Nui in 1774, he discovered broken, toppled statues and skeletal remains near some of the ceremonial platforms (ahu), *suggesting that the violent breakdown of the island's culture was underway. Engraving by expedition artist William Hodges.*

especially) had been concealed there while strangers were on hand, thus accounting for abrupt population shifts. These caves played an important role in island life: as shelter from the elements, safe storage for family valuables, burial chambers, and protection from enemies during times of civil strife.

Above: Two-headed birdman figure portrayed on a tapa-*cloth sail for the* Rapa Nui *film. Facing page: The features of the* moai *are monumental and exaggerated; some see the heads, with their long jutting noses and protruding lips, as sexual symbols.*

One thing is certain: no new *moai* were constructed after the era of outside contact began, and the heyday of their creation was well past by then. We will return later on to the decline and fall of Rapa Nui's classic culture and what may have led to it, and briefly trace the islanders' fortunes from the nineteenth century to the present. It's not a happy tale. The Dutch farewell, with a dozen islanders shot to death in a dispute over stolen property, was only the first of many abuses the islanders suffered at the hands of outsiders.

After a long period of exploitation, Rapa Nui began to see some benefits from the civilized world, in the form of improved living conditions, medicine, and income from tourism. But as Paul Bahn and John Flenley point out, "the present-day Easter Islanders live amid the ruins of their ancestors' remarkable accomplishments." It is Rapa Nui's vanished ancient culture that has fascinated all who have come there, and continues to fas-

1769 drawing by Sydney Parkinson of a Polynesian double canoe from the Society Islands, with shelters on deck for long-distance voyaging.

The Star Voyagers

The people of Polynesia's far-flung realms have always been gifted and daring seafarers. Since ancient times, the sea was their element; these island cultures lived off its bounty and regularly paddled to and fro in their home archipelagoes, to trade and socialize with neighboring islands, sometimes to make war on them.

They also undertook amazing long-distance voyages of colonization. By around 3200 B.C., settlers had reached the western Polynesian isles of Tonga and Samoa from Melanesia, and in these rich, comfortable islands honed the navigation skills that would eventually carry them nearly all the way across the Pacific. Their main techniques were tracking star paths—they recognized and used hundreds of stars—and an almost magical sensitivity to surface currents and wave forms. David Lewis notes, "The skilled navigator comes to recognize the profile and characteristics of particular ocean swells as he would the faces of his friends." Sometimes they would get into the water and test the current's strength on the body's most sensitive skin: the scrotum. By observing seabirds, changes in the wind and swells, clouds that gather over land, and bioluminescence in the water, they could sense the proximity of land long before it was visible.

Their distinctive double canoes could carry dozens of passengers and tons of supplies, allowing them to remain for weeks at sea. They were rigged to sail into the wind if need be, but the voyagers more often relied on their knowledge of when the prevailing southeast trades gave way to westerlies—the El Niño phenomenon—thus enabling them to sail east with ease. The canoes were also built for speed; Captain Cook reported that Tongan chiefs could sail rings around his ship.

Emboldened by ever-growing knowledge and experience, they steadily expanded their range of travel. "Over the centuries," write Bahn and Flenley, "it is probable that a faith was born that there were always new lands to be found: eastward, ever eastward."

The last of those lands to be discovered was Rapa Nui—and it's still debated whether the first colonists arrived by accident or on a purposeful mission of settlement. Although some colonizations were preceded by a scouting voyage, it's unlikely that so tiny and isolated a speck as Rapa Nui would be found twice, even by skilled sailors. Most probably, Hotu Matua and company were on their way somewhere, bearing all the needs for a new colony, but missed their destination or strayed south out of the tradewinds belt, encountering the westerlies that took them to the island. Once there, "far from the mainstream of Polynesian voyaging," they were to remain "the most isolated of colonies, largely or totally cut off from the rest of Polynesia."

cinate us. Let's move back in time and take a closer look at the original inhabitants—Hotu Matua's people—and the place where they landed.

Rapa Nui's sunsets are among the most memorable to be found in the Pacific isles.

Where Did They Come From?

In recounting tales of their origins, most Easter Islanders have spoken of a large, warm island or group of islands somewhere to the west, from where Hotu Matua embarked, sailing toward the sunrise to land on Rapa Nui. These folk memories are far from consistent, however. Some claim that Hotu Matua was the first human to set foot on the island; others say that his brother Machaa scouted the way and arrived two months earlier. Hotu Matua's homeland has been variously named as Marae Renga, Marae Tohio, or Hiva. And some stories reversed the direction of travel, declaring that Hotu Matua sailed *from* the land of the rising sun rather than toward it—in other words, came from the east.

This version of things was seized on by Thor Heyerdahl in his long-running attempt to prove that Rapa Nui's first settlers came from South America, and belonged to a sophisticated pre-Inca culture. Heyerdahl's belief grew out of his famous 1947 *Kon-Tiki* expedition—a dramatic three-month drift voyage in a balsa-wood sail-rigged raft, heading out from the Peruvian coast to a shipwreck landing in the Tuamotus, east of Tahiti. Easter Island became part of his overall quest to prove that Polynesia could have been visited or settled by Amerindians. After the *Kon-Tiki* adventure, Heyerdahl visited the island in 1955 with a team of archeologists and set about gathering data to prove his pre-formed conclusion; this expedition resulted in the book *Aku-Aku: The Secret of Easter Island*.

That Amerindians could have reached Easter Island from Peru was supposedly demonstrated by the *Kon-Tiki*'s success in exploiting the prevailing southeasterly winds to drift westward toward Polynesia. This demands an imaginative leap, however, since Heyerdahl's raft was equipped with advantages unknown to Peru's coastal culture in the early

Petroglyphs of fertility symbols on the cliffs of Poike, above the original "white virgin" caves.

Bone fish hooks found on Easter Island (below left) were often made of human thigh bones and similar to hooks found elsewhere in Polynesia (drawings at center and right).

centuries A.D.: a radio, solar still, navigation gear, maps, and sails—the latter used by Peruvians only after the Spanish introduced them. Moreover, the *Kon-Tiki* had to be towed 50 miles out to sea to escape coastal currents that otherwise would have carried it north. And, of course, Heyerdahl knew in advance that islands lay to the west, which early Peruvians did not. In fact, no good evidence exists for an Amerindian culture making long ocean voyages, regardless of favorable winds.

The Polynesians, on the other hand, were experienced open-ocean travelers, fanning out from their southeast Asian origins to colonize virtually every island in the South Pacific over a 30 million-square-mile span—"the great seafaring saga of all time," as one writer put it. Despite Rapa Nui's remote and isolated location, it is far more reasonable to assume that it could have been reached by Polynesians from the west—probably from the Marquesas, evidence suggests—than by coast-hugging Peruvians from the east. Whether it was a skillfully navigated voyage, like other Polynesian colonizing expeditions, or a lucky accident remains a mystery.

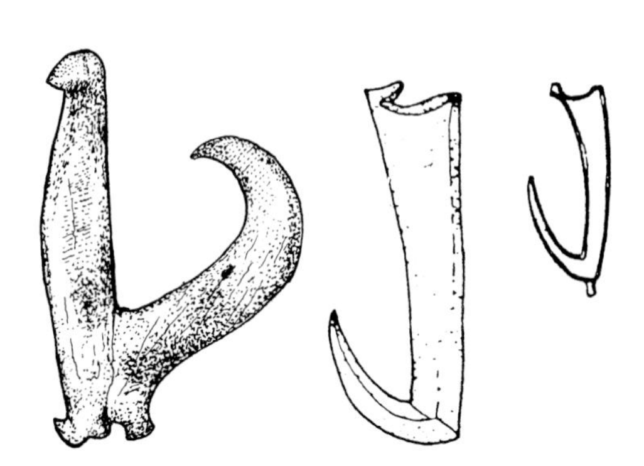

Heyerdahl's daring voyages, prolific writings, and flair for publicity have made him one of the best-known adventurers of this century. His ideas have captured the public's imagination and compelled scholars to examine all their assumptions about Rapa Nui closely. However, the results of thirty years of detailed study in archeology, physical anthropology, and related work in linguistics and botany have only strengthened their primary assumption—that Rapa Nui was indeed first settled by Polynesians from the west. Any links between the island and the South American mainland remain tenuous and unproven.

« I had asked the captain to steer around the north coast to get a general impression of most of the island before landing. We were gliding along a perpendicular cliff where foaming breakers had eaten their way into the volcanic formation till the coast was sheer and immensely high. There were gleams of reddish-brown and yellowish-gray as in the layers of a cut cake, and high up on the crest over our heads we could see green grass and ancient walls which seemed on the verge of tumbling down the precipice. Mile followed mile of inaccessible cliffs, till the surface of the island changed shape and rolled its stone-strewn fields down toward the sea from round grassy hummocks and hillocks in the interior. The green never came right down to the surf, for there a tumbled barrier of black lava blocks lay like a protecting wall all round the island. Only at one place did the landscape really open up, and there the island smiled at us, revealing a broad sunlit beach. The whole effect was wonderfully beautiful and inviting. »

Thor Heyerdahl
Aku-Aku: The Secret of Easter Island

In analyzing Rapa Nui's artifacts and architecture, Heyerdahl found or stretched parallels with South American cultures wherever possible, while ignoring evidence that didn't fit his theory. Rapa Nui's only tools were stone and bone: primitive adzes and picks for woodcutting and stone-carving, bone fish hooks. All are recognizably Polynesian in form and development. Much attention has been paid to the ceremonial platforms (*ahu*) built of large, well-fitted, mortarless stone blocks; Heyerdahl's claim that "Polynesian fisherman" could not have built them is weakened by other examples of fine stonework on some of the Marquesas, Tonga, and Hawaii. As for the giant *moai*, they have confounded all attempts to trace their ancestry, bearing scant resemblance to sculpture found either on the mainland or in Polynesia. Like other extraordinary manifestations of long-isolated cultures, they seem to be *sui generis.*

Further evidence of Rapa Nui's Polynesian roots has emerged from painstaking studies of human blood types, bone structure, and linguistic affinities, as well as plant pollen that can be dated back thousands of years. Most scientists—even those who accompanied Heyerdahl to the island in 1955—agree that "most of what is known of the prehistoric culture... suggests Polynesian immigrants from islands to the west." Still, Heyerdahl's enthusiastic efforts did open up a new era of scientific research on Rapa Nui.

Long Ears and Short Ears

A persistent legend on Rapa Nui—and a central plot device of the film—is that its population was for centuries divided into two groups: the *Hanau Eepe* and the *Hanau Momoko*, often translated as "Long Ears" and "Short Ears." The practice of artificially lengthening the earlobes and inserting ornaments in them was common on Rapa Nui for at least part of its history. Drawings of islanders by early European visitors show them, and indeed, the *moai* themselves have elongated ears, matching the rest of their exaggerated features.

The source and meaning of this distinction have sparked much controversy. Thor Heyerdahl took the Long Ear phenomenon as evidence that Rapa Nui's first settlers were of South American origin, where some pre-Incas distended their earlobes with stone plugs. He accepts an island tradition that the Short Ears were a laboring class subservient to the Long Ear chiefs, until they revolted and killed all but one Long Ear, then overthrew the statues. (See sidebar "The Battle at Poike Ditch," page 49) The so-called Short Ears, according to Heyerdahl, may have been Polynesians who settled on Rapa Nui some time after the "Amerindian" Long Ears were already in residence.

Contrary to Heyerdahl's claim, however, ear-lengthening occurs here and there in Polynesia—and there is no evidence that Rapa Nui experienced more than one wave of settlement. Moreover, it's probable that *Hanau Eepe* and *Hanau Momoko* have been mistranslated: experts insist that the terms actually meant "stocky people" and "slender people," respectively. This would make sense based on the Polynesian association of bulkiness with *mana* and the aristocracy. That conflict arose between groups of islanders at some point is likely...that they were of different ethnic origin is not.

Engraving by William Hodges of an Easter Islander with stretched earlobes, c. 1774.

Heyerdahl's ideas have the power of imagination and conviction, and he was unafraid to rely on native legends when it suited his purpose. Admitting the predominant Polynesian influence in Rapa Nui's later history, he still insisted that they were latecomers to the island, perhaps even brought there by more sophisticated "slave traders" from South America. This dovetailed neatly with an island legend of two ancient classes: an aristocracy known as "Long Ears" for their habit of stretching the earlobes, and the working-class "Short Ears." This notion could be spun out in many directions; for example, that the Long Ears were the masterminds of the *moai* while the Short Ears just did the grunt work.

Unproved speculation is far more entertaining than the cautious progress of science, and Easter Island is the kind of place that encourages the imagination to run wild. The Swiss writer Erich Von Däniken

Part of the giant Rano Kau crater, in the island's southwest corner, one of its three extinct volcanoes. Overleaf: Rano Raraku, the crater where the moai *were quarried, from the outside.*

claimed that aliens from other worlds must have made and erected the great statues; Atlantis fans see the island as the last fragment of a sunken continent (it is, to the contrary, surrounded by great ocean deeps). Heyerdahl's science is stronger than these flights of fancy, but he tended to rely overmuch on local myths—as unreliable on Easter Island as anywhere else—and to build his theoretical pyramids upside-down. In his enthusiasm for Amerindian cultures he gives the impression that the Polynesians were somehow inferior in their capabilities. That they were indeed capable of the monumental achievements on Rapa Nui has been established without doubt.

The Island They Found

"After sailing for two months in the open sea," writes Paul Theroux of the Polynesians who discovered Rapa Nui, "the voyagers came upon the island and they sailed completely around it, looking for a place to land. After their tropical home, this windy...island must have seemed a forbidding place; then, as now, black cliffs being beaten by surf. They found the island's only bay, its only sandy beach. They went ashore there and named the bay Anakena, their word for the month of August.

Above: Palm trees much larger than these probably grew on Rapa Nui once, a species related to the Chilean wine palm. Below: Palm frond petrolglyph from the island.

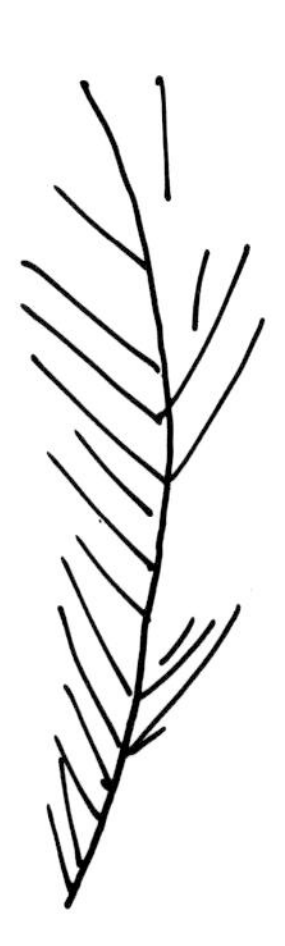

It was an island of seabirds and grass. There were no mammals. The craters of the volcanoes were filled with *totora* reeds."

At 27 degrees latitude (about the same distance from the Equator as northern Florida), Rapa Nui is the most southerly of the Polynesian isles and does not share their celebrated balmy climate. The mean annual temperature is about 69°F; high winds and frequent storms are a fact of life. Offshore, too, cooler temperatures mean that reef-forming corals do not grow well, so the coastline is unprotected. Even on a normal day, Pacific swells that have journeyed thousands of miles crash against the cliffs with daunting ferocity.

Rapa Nui is a volcanic island, with cratered peaks near each corner of its triangular shape. Formed in a typical way, by violent eruptions from a "hot spot" in the ocean floor, the entire island is actually just the top 3,000 feet of a mountain 10,000 feet high and mostly submerged. It is probably still an active volcano somewhere far below, though no surface eruptions have occurred since the era of human habitation began.

Though it's hard to imagine now, at the time of the first settlers the island probably was covered by scrubby forest. Even then it lacked the lush vegetation of most Polynesian landscapes, and today Rapa Nui is clothed mainly in grasses. There are frequent rocky outcrops and areas of rubble-strewn soil, barely weathered from the volcanic rock. All the usual kinds of volcanic rock are present, from relatively soft tuff, formed of compressed ash—the raw material of the *moai* —to much harder basalt and obsidian, used for building blocks, hand tools, and weapons. Another notable feature of the volcanic landscape is a vast network of lava tubes all around the island, formed when lava continues to flow under the surface after the top layer has cooled and set. These are the famous caves that have figured prominently in Easter Island's history.

> **« We have found it...outstandingly fruitful, producing bananas, sweet potatoes, sugar-cane of special thickness, and many other sorts of produce, although devoid of large trees and livestock, apart from fowls, so this land, because of its rich earth and good climate, could be made into an earthly Paradise if it was properly cultivated and worked, which at present is done only to the extent that the inhabitants are required to for maintenance of life. »**
>
> Jacob Roggeveen
> *Journals*

Only forty-six native plant species were counted by a botanist in 1956. Some plants may have been wiped out by human impact, but probably the island's environment has always been limited in diversity, because of its extreme isolation. The only way for plants to arrive there was by wind-borne spores, seeds floating on the water, or—the most common way for new plants to reach remote islands—stuck to the feet and feathers of seabirds. Of course the human settlers brought with them several food crops—sweet potatoes, bananas, and sugarcane—as well as some ornamentals.

The lack of vegetation—especially large woody trees—was remarked by the earliest outsiders; the Dutch captain Roggeveen described the island as "destitute of large trees." Indeed, this is among the island's chief mysteries, since the climate is reasonably hospitable to tree growth, and the soils rich enough in most places to support them. Even before the later time of social turmoil and rapid deforestation, pollen studies indicate that the island's flora was relatively poor in variety. Factors in the slow, long-range transformation of the island's plant life probably include low rainfall (with periods of extreme drought), high winds, the lack of surface streams, and human impacts such as tree-cutting and burning to clear land for agriculture.

Lakes that formed within the craters of Rano Kau, Rano Aroi, and Rano Raraku were once the island's chief source of fresh water, and they also supported a more lush plant growth than elsewhere. Now reduced to swamps through overuse, they still harbor many species. The

The Birdmen of Easter Island

The Birdman ritual emerged late in Rapa Nui's pre-contact history. The only record—a list of some 86 sacred Birdmen ending in 1866—suggests it might have begun as late as the mid-1700s, but some think it is older.

The annual race to Motu Nui is linked with the worship of the creator god Make-Make, whose cult supplanted ancestor reverence on the island. Its object was to choose a new Birdman to be Make-Make's representative on earth. The candidates, usually ambitious chiefs of dominant clans, did not compete themselves but chose athletic young subordinates for the grueling and dangerous race. They had to clamber down the 1,000-foot cliff that forms the edge of the Rano Kau volcano to a rocky scrap of beach at the bottom, and swim more than a mile out in the rough seas on floats made of lashed-together *totora* reeds to the islet of Motu Nui, where the sooty terns nested.

The first to find an egg held it aloft and called to his chief, watching with a crowd from the ceremonial village of Orongo on the clifftop: "Shave your head...you have got the egg!" (By tradition the winner had all the hair on his head and face shaved, while the losers cut themselves with obsidian *mataa* blades.)

Photo shows the bas-relief carving typical of later birdman petroglyphs; drawings show simple early designs that evolved into the bas-relief style.

But the winner was not known for sure until the contestants—eggs tucked into a headband rig—swam back and ascended the cliff. The first chief to have an intact egg delivered into his hand became the Birdman, and went off to live in seclusion for the next year at a special house near the foot of Rano Raraku.

totora reed, from which the islanders made small rafts and swimming floats, is abundant there. This plant figured in the controversy over the origins of the Rapanui: Thor Heyerdahl claimed that it must have been brought from South America, where it grows in many lakes. But the latest pollen studies prove the Easter Island variety is more than 30,000 years old, long predating any human arrival.

Native fauna is even rarer. No mammals are native to the island, though the Polynesian rat has been there as long as humans have, brought along by them as a food source. Sheep, pigs, horses, and cattle were all introduced in the late nineteenth century, and are still part of the island's economy. The only land birds—small hawks, partridge, and quail—were introduced, as was the chicken, which thrived to become

A frigate bird on Moto Nui islet, one of about 30 brought there for the film and released. The cliffs of mainland Rapa Nui are in the distance.

the island's staple protein. There are plenty of insects and other invertebrates, though some of these too were imported.

Migratory seabirds used to nest on the island in great numbers; these included petrels, frigate birds, boobies, and various terns. The sooty tern—known locally as the "sunbird"— featured in one of Rapa Nui's traditional rituals, the annual race to choose the Birdman. Each springtime (that is, September) young men representing the chiefs of the ruling clans competed to be the first to retrieve an egg laid by the nesting terns from the islet of Motu Nui, off the island's southwestern

A major set for the film re-created a seventeenth-century Rapa Nui village, with its reed huts shaped like inverted canoes.

cape. The winner's chief became the Birdman for the following year; his privileges included living at ease while others labored for him. Frigate birds, with their large hooked beaks, are prominently depicted in the island's many petroglyphs of "birdmen"—literally a human figure with a bird's head.

The embracing ocean was a vital resource for Rapa Nui's Polynesian immigrants, though the absence of a coral reef meant that fewer species of fish and shellfish were available than elsewhere in the South Pacific. Marine mammals were not abundant around the island, or at least were

not extensively hunted by the settlers, judging from archeological evidence. Nor were turtles, although some are seen in petroglyph carvings, and decorative objects were made from their shells. Possibly the islanders' boats were not stout enough to hunt very large fish or whales in the rough seas around Rapa Nui. Other species like seals and sea lions tend to colonize islands closer to mainland shores.

All in all, it was a land of meager resources that the followers of Hotu Matua found at the end of their voyage. Nonetheless they settled in, cleared land, planted their crops, and started building—and kept on building. They seem to have had no thought of leaving; at least there is no evidence that they ever reached another inhabited land from Rapa Nui. Probably it did not seem a viable option: the memory of their original journey must have been harrowing, and the seas around the island did not encourage long-range voyaging. (Rarely did the islanders venture beyond sight of land even to fish.) So there they remained in solitude, for perhaps 1,400 years. What was their life on Rapa Nui like?

Living in the Ancestors' Shadows

We don't know who Hotu Matua really was—the name simply means "Great Parent" or "Prolific Father." Certainly the Easter Island immigrants were led by some notable personage, a member of an aristocratic Polynesian family who had a good reason to relocate. Motives included natural disasters such as earthquakes, volcanic events, or tidal waves; warfare and violent family disputes; or involuntary exile. Some colonizers were the youngers sons of chiefs who left home to make their fortunes because the first-born always inherited the family land. Others were strong, ambitious men who posed a threat to the local rulers.

The great double canoes used for colonizing voyages could hold up

Carving on a moai *apparently shows a European ship with a turtle.*

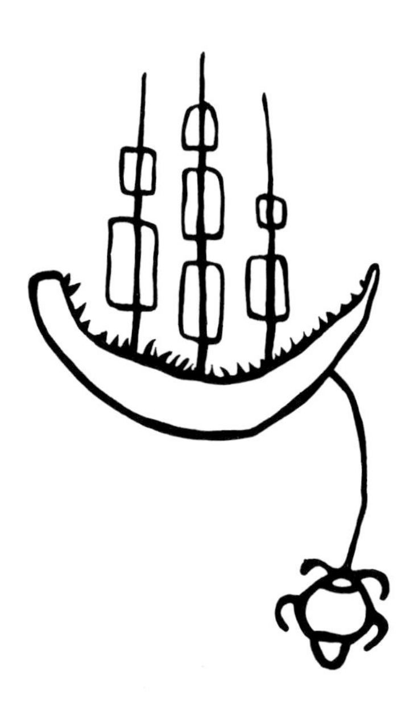

to several dozen people. The passengers would likely have included one or more members of a priestly clan, who could invoke the aid of gods and ancestors; relatives of the leader; perhaps a specialist in tattooing, which was practiced widely in Oceania. Certainly there would have been a navigator, who possessed highly developed and closely guarded skills, passed down to selected initiates. For the rest: men and women chosen because they were good workers, or who had loyalties that led them to join their leader in seeking a new life.

Their earliest settlements clustered around the southwest corner of Rapa Nui, near the present-day population center of Hanga Roa. Eventually the settlers spread out to occupy nearly all the coastal regions, living in small groups of two or three dwellings surrounded by agricultural land. Fewer people lived inland, though some areas were farmed or exploited for natural springs.

"There were also," write Paul Bahn and John Flenley, "village complexes, clustered around a religious/ceremonial site with its altar platform, and [about] 165 to 330 feet away, five or more elliptical houses for priests, chiefs or other people of high rank. Commoners' dwellings stood a further 330 to 660 feet inland from these elite structures."

Photo shows a partly reconstructed hare paenga *(elliptical house), with ends of the branch framework inserted in holes in the foundation stones. Drawing shows a finished house with its paved terrace outside.*

Most of the islanders lived in boat-shaped houses made of reeds attached to a framework of branches. In ordinary homes the branches were simply stuck into the ground, but the homes of the more important had foundations made of cut basalt blocks. Some of these structures were large enough to hold several families, and at least one could shelter more than a hundred people. The remains of houses built entirely of stone, with thick walls and corbelled roofs, have been found, and caves were also used as dwellings. Sometimes these were "improved" with further underground excavation, entrance ramps, and doorways; others were merely temporary shelters used by fishermen along the coast.

The interior of the house was mainly for sleeping; cooking—and most other daily activities—took place outside. Stone-lined underground ovens, called *umu pae*, are

In the ceremonial village of Orongo, between the cliffs and Rano Kau crater, are the remains of some 50 thick-walled houses built of basalt slabs with corbelled roofs. They are thought to date from the late 16th century.

found all over the island, its most common archeological features. Some of the more impressive houses had a paved "patio" outside for domestic work and socializing. Basalt was also used to construct chicken houses (*hare moa*) and garden enclosures, safeguarding these important food resources.

Unlike most Polynesian cultures, Rapa Nui was more dependent on agriculture than fishing for sustenance. Crops such as sweet potatoes and bananas were easy to grow in abundance. Fishing was certainly important, especially on the island's northern and western coasts, and people gathered shellfish everywhere they could. But lacking any reef-protected lagoons, which encourage large-scale cooperative netting, the islanders relied more on line fishing and the use of smaller nets. Over the centuries, due to a growing shortage of wood for seaworthy canoes, they apparently lost the ability to venture far offshore after deepwater fish and were restricted to inshore fishing. Ordinary folk had to beware of taking fish that were declared *tapu*—reserved for clan leaders.

Along with their worldly goods, the first settlers brought with them basic Polynesian patterns of social life and structure. At first they were probably all linked, by blood ties or obligation, to a single strong chief. As time went by, rival clans emerged and staked out various parts of the

island as their territories, building settlements around the great ceremonial platforms known as *ahu*. By the sixteenth century, certain high-status members of each clan—"chiefs, priests, possessors of ritual knowledge and arts, and the warriors," as Bahn and Flenley note, were living off the labor of a much larger underclass. Yet until very near the end of the pre-contact era there was remarkably little warfare, either between rival clans or social classes. Such relative harmony is atypical of ancient Polynesian societies; it may reflect the urgent need for cooperation in their isolated circumstances, or the unifying power of common beliefs.

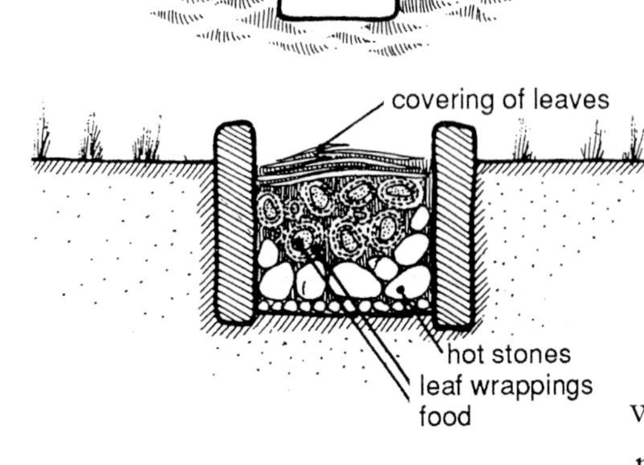

Ancestor worship is practiced throughout Polynesia. Ceremonial platforms called *marae* are a common feature of its island civilizations, as are carvings representing ancestors—usually of wood, though stone statues are found in the Marquesas and elsewhere. "The deifying of great men who were either direct descendants of the gods, mighty warriors, or people with great prestige was a deeply rooted characteristic of

Polynesian culture," notes Paul Bahn.

Nowhere else, however, did the worship of ancestors take the form it did on Easter Island: that of a stupendous communal building enterprise. Both literally and figuratively, Hotu Matua cast a long shadow over his descendants. The image of this original ancestor is kept alive through myth in the minds of present-day islanders—and perhaps also in the visages of the giant *moai* quarried over the centuries and erected on *ahus* ringing the island's perimeter. How and why this was done is the most thoroughly investigated of all Rapa Nui's mysteries, and it is still not fully solved.

« We know from the island's ethnography that there were restrictions (*tapu*) on marine resources, which were controlled by the high- status Miru clan of the north; this explains why most petroglyphs not only of fish-hooks but also of sea creatures are located on the north coast. The island's highest chief redistributed the prestige fish (a common phenomenon in Polynesia), while resources of great economic value, such as tuna, turtles, seals and dolphins, were reserved exclusively for the aristocracy at certain times. Only the Miru nobles could continue to enjoy larger fish like tuna during the *tapu* months from May to October, and lesser mortals would supposedly be poisoned or develop asthma if they too tried to eat them then.... »

Paul Bahn and John Flenley
Easter Island, Earth Island

Moai and *Mana*

A row of giant statues representing primitive gods, all alike as cookies from a cutter, their eyeless faces staring endlessly out to sea...

This has been the popular image of the Easter Island *moai*, as depicted in cartoons and pulp journalism. It promotes several misconceptions. The statues actually were built to honor the memory and conserve the power of high-ranking ancestors, not to incarnate local deities. Though similar in general form, they varied considerably from one to the next in size, shape, and expression. Although they have been eyeless for many years, they were originally fitted with large staring eyes of white coral, red scoria, and black obsidian, making their gaze both more human and more powerful. (The eyes may not have been permanent but inserted only on special occasions.) Finally, the figures did not face out to sea but *inland*, looking out over the day-to-day activities and ceremonial events of their makers.

Facing page, top: Petroglyphs including a palm frond and fertility symbol in a cave at Ana o Keke, on the Poike peninsula. Bottom: Top and cross-section view of an earth oven (umu pae), *lined with cut basalt slabs.*

The *moai* seem to have evolved from an earlier practice of carving smaller statues in a more naturalistic style. It's not known for sure when the first of the "classic" *moai* was created, though the oldest one found on a platform dates back to the twelfth century. Most likely they were being made before this. The last known statue was carved in A.D. 1650, so for at least half a millennium their creation was a ruling passion on Rapa Nui.

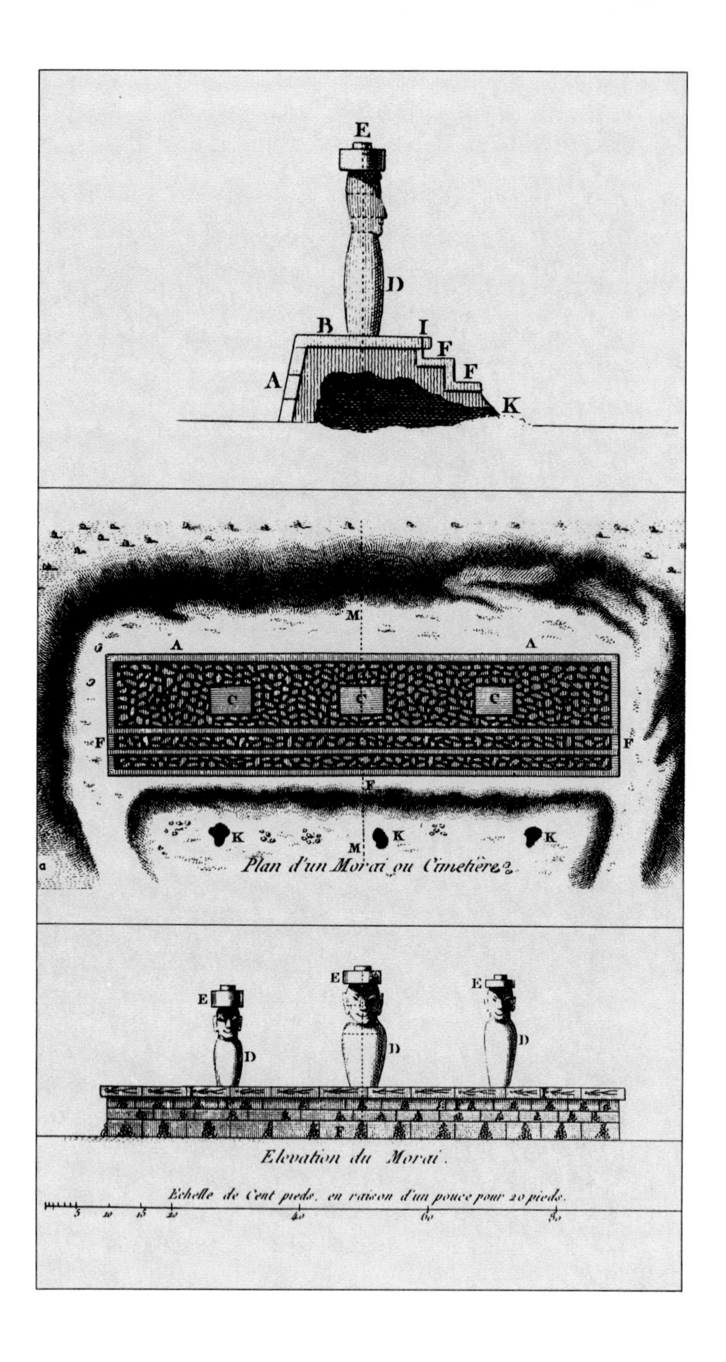

Architectural renderings of an ahu by M. Bernizet, the engineer of the French 1786 expedition led by La Pérouse. The foundation contained a burial chamber.

The statues themselves are so amazing that people tend to overlook the equally impressive platforms on which they stand. More than 250 *ahu* ring the island, occupying the heart of every settlement as well as uninhabited sites. Made of a core of rubble faced with masonry, they were sometimes used as burial chambers, though cremation of high-ranking folk was more common in the early period of the culture, and exposure or cave burial later on. Some of the outer walls were made of huge basalt blocks precisely cut and fitted, equal to the best mortarless masonry in the world; others were more casually constructed. However large or elaborate, they clearly served as the foci for all ceremonial activity and to elevate still higher the images of the revered ancestors.

The finished statues on platforms range from 6 to 33 feet high. The largest ever carved was a staggering 65 feet long, but it was never raised from its bed of stone in the quarry. Most are strikingly similar, at least at first glance: a columnar figure shown down to the abdomen, the head huge and angular with highly stylized facial features, the earlobes distended, the arms held close to the body with elongated fingers resting on the belly. Many have bas-relief designs on their backs that resemble the intricate tattoos seen in many parts of the Pacific. Most at one time wore "hats" of red scoria, another local stone. These cylindrical headpieces, hoisted up onto the statues' heads after they were erected, probably represent a topknot style of hair-dressing rather than hats.

Reams have been written about the engineering marvel that the *moai* represent for a Stone Age culture—how they might have been carved, possible techniques for transporting them to and raising them on the *ahu*. A brief summary will have to suffice here. Virtually all the statues were carved at an enormous, sloping-sided quarry in the Rano Raraku crater. Several hundred were at one time or another transported out to sites around the island; several hundred more remain—in broken fragments, buried up to the neck, or as partially carved embryo *moai*—in the quarry

Ancient moai *on the Ahu Tahai; the farther statue has been restored with its* pukao *headdress and eyes.*

itself, one of the world's most evocative archeological sites. Others have been found scattered here and there along probable transport routes to *ahu* sites.

The most common misconception about the *moai* is that people equipped only with stone hand tools could never have carved the "steel-hard volcanic stone" of which they are formed. (The description is Erich Von Däniken's, who insisted that extraterrestrials must have made them.) But in fact, the statues are steel-hard only on the outer surfaces exposed to weather; inside, the tuff can be cut fairly easily with stone tools, especially if it is softened with water while being worked. Experiments by Thor Heyerdahl and others suggest that a team of about twenty experienced carvers could have completed even the largest *moai* within a year. Many such teams were probably at work simultaneously,

> « What is certain is that specialized master-craftsmen were at work here; the islanders reported that the sculptors had been a privileged class, their craft being hereditary in the male line, and that it was a matter of great pride to be a member of a sculptor's family. According to legend, the statue carvers were relieved of all other work, so that the fishermen and farmers had to provide them with food, especially valuable seafood... »
>
> Paul Bahn and John Flenley
> *Easter Island, Earth Island*

turning the quarry into a hive of hammering, dust, and sweat.

The figures were carved lying on their backs, usually pointing downhill to facilitate moving them later on. The procedure began with a master designer roughing out the shape of the finished statue on the rock. Then the pounding began—countless hours of countless blows with pointed basalt picks called *poki*, thousands of which have been found in the crater. They went dull quickly, so new ones had to be constantly supplied, along with water to wet the tuff. As the figure emerged from the surrounding rock, it was left anchored to the bedrock by a narrow strip of stone along the spine, a sort of "keel." This was pierced with holes at intervals, and when they were ready to move the finished *moai*, the remaining spans of rock were broken away.

The second great technical question is how the *moai* were lowered from their birthing places high up on the slope of the crater, and then transported to their destinations atop the *ahu*—sometimes miles across the island. Apparently the workers used a system of ropes, tree-trunk posts, and (in some places) stone "bollards" to take the weight of the statue once it was set free of its moorings, and then carefully lower it downslope via shallow channels in the ground. The ropes, woven from the fibrous bark of a native shrub known as *hauhau*, were a critical element in lowering the statues, levering them upright onto sledges for long-distance movement, and finally erecting them in place on the *ahu*. (See the sidebar "Making the *Moai* Walk" on page 42 for more details on statue transport.)

> **« Their size would have been overwhelming enough, even if they had been badly carved. But these were brilliantly executed, with long sloping noses and pursed lips and sharp chins. Their ears were elongated, and the hands clasping the body had long fingers, the sort you see on certain elegant Buddhas. Some of the statues had a mass of intricate detail on their backs. And although there was some similarity among the statues' profiles, each one had a distinctly different face. »**
>
> Paul Theroux
> *The Happy Isles of Oceania*

Facing page: In the Rano Raraku quarry, many unfinished or abandoned moai *have been partly buried by centuries of windblown soil. Below: Diagram of how the statues were carved out of the rock, leaving a perforated keel.*

But more fascinating than any of the islanders' feats of engineering is the deeper question of *why* the statues were made. It is really an interlocking chain of questions: Given that they felt compelled, like other Polynesians, to honor their ancestors, why did they choose to make figures in stone rather the more typical wood carvings? Why make them so huge and so uniform; why line them up at the edge of the sea? Why keep on making them for century after century, devoting so much of the population's labor force to the task? Why do they look as they do?

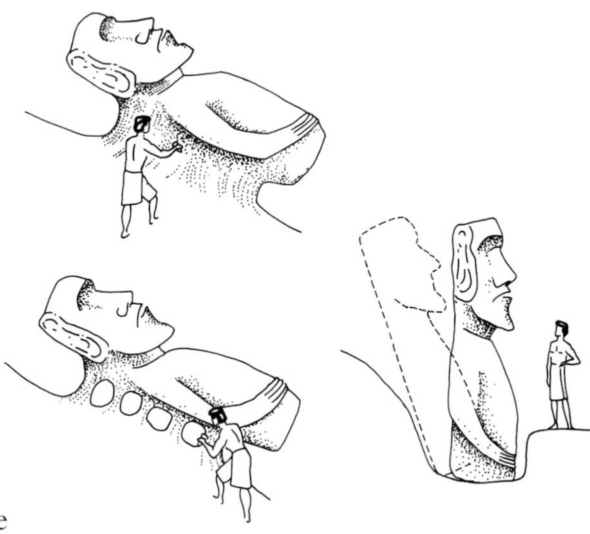

One large clue to these mysteries may be the extreme remoteness of Easter Island, and how unlike other Polynesian lands it is. The place the settlers found at the end of their eastward journey was no reef-sheltered tropical paradise, rich in hardwood forests. It was a windswept piece of rock that must have seemed as if the sea could swallow it at any time. There were trees, but few very suitable for the intricate woodcarving they were used to. On the other hand, there was stone everywhere. One of the immigrants' first

Making the *Moai* Walk

I turned...to the native shepherd who stood by me in silence gazing at the abandoned giants which lay about on the plain.

"Leonardo," I said, "you are a practical man. Can you tell me how these stone giants could have been carried about in old times?"

"They went of themselves," Leonardo replied.

But for his grave, almost reverent air I should have thought he was joking...

"But, Leonardo," I said, "how could they go when they had only heads and bodies and no legs?"

"They wriggled along like this," said Leonardo, and gave a demonstration by working himself along the rock with feet together and stiff knees. "How do you think it happened?" he asked indulgently.

This incident from Thor Heyerdahl's *Aku-Aku* dramatizes one of the chief mysteries of the *moai*: how they were moved from the Rano Raraku quarry to various sites all over the island. The more farfetched explanations include electromagnetic or antigravity forces, extraterrestrial intervention, and a theory that they were roughed out in the quarry,

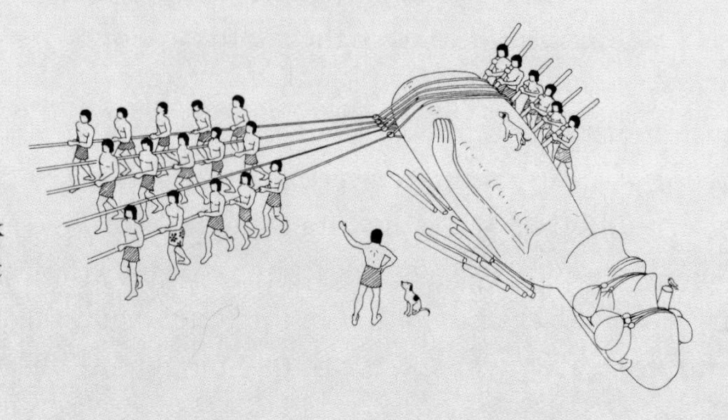

Facing page, top: Filmed depiction of the Monster moai *being gradually tilted upright onto log rollers. Bottom: How some of the statues might have been moved by the "canoe-swivel" method. Left: Closeup of the palm-log sledge made for the film.*

blown from erupting volcanoes like acrobats from a circus cannon, and finished on the platforms where they landed!

Serious researchers, including Heyerdahl, start from the premise that the ancient islanders—lacking any equipment but logs, stones, bark rope, and brute strength—nonetheless accomplished these feats without supernatural aid. Archeologists have conducted painstaking experiments to deduce what techniques might have been used

Traditional islanders like Leonardo resorted to a mythical explanation: the *moai* simply walked by themselves, propelled by spiritual power. After hearing the same tale from many of them, Heyerdahl started thinking about what factual roots it might have. He and others speculated that some kind of tilt-and-swivel method was used to move the statues in an upright position—rather like "walking" a refrigerator to and fro across a floor—with ropes around its neck to pull and guide it. Experiments by Czech engineer Pavel Pavel showed this was possible but problematic, and damaged the statues' bases.

Another method, suggested by archeologist William Mulloy, involves fitting the statue with a Y-shaped fork from a tree, lowering it to a prone position with ropes, and rocking it forward on its stomach in small increments, levered by a set of shearlegs. This too had serious drawbacks, including the lack of suitable trees. Still another occurred to the French archeologist Jean-Pierre Adam, from watching fishermen move a canoe up a beach by swiveling it end to end with a roller log placed underneath. The same principle, with more complex mechanics, could be applied to moving the *moai*.

The most likely technique, proposed by American geologist Charles Love, was that the statue was first elevated onto a wooden sledge, which was then dragged over a series of log rollers to the *ahu*, where the statue was positioned with help from the tilt-and-swivel method. Just getting the *moai* upright was a large task: men with log levers would raise the top end inches at a time, allowing others to stuff stones, and more stones, underneath—eventually forming a ramp the workers climbed up as the statue tilted skyward. A similar ramp-building technique may have been used to raise some of the statues onto platforms.

Another intriguing possibility is that some statues, as well as large stone blocks for building *ahus*, were transported the short 500 meters from the quarry to the coast, and ferried on rafts to their destinations. The remains of ancient *apapa*, or stone canoe-ramps, make this idea plausible.

As Paul Bahn observes, no one method would have worked for all the statues. Depending on their size and destination, and the resources available, various means were surely used.

Above: Closeup of recreated moai *heads with eyes and/or headdresses. Facing page: Small* kavakava *figures, carved from the native* toro-miro *and later from imported woods, have been seen since Captain Cook's visit. They always depict a thin, stooped man with prominent ribs, probably harking to the time when the island began experiencing food shortages.*

tasks was simply to move massive amounts of loose stone to clear land for planting; it would have been natural enough to pile them into heaps that became landmarks, later refined into ceremonial platforms. Making images in stone probably started on a small scale, and escalated through competition to larger and more impressive versions.

As to how the islanders could devote so much time to the endeavor, Bahn and Flenley observe that "in prehistoric times—and particularly on a small isolated island—there was little else to do." Raising or catching enough food was not an all-consuming task by any means, especially since Rapa Nui offered scant opportunity for the kind of large-scale subsistence projects carried out elsewhere in Polynesia, like netfishing or irrigated farming. Even when food grew scarce, however, the building continued, at this point taking on the tinge of an obsession.

The most important function of the statues, as objects of veneration, was to incorporate the *mana* of their models—the power or spirit force of the great person they represent. Some believe that Hotu Matua is in a sense the original model for all the *moai*, the "ancestor of ancestors," the Great Parent of all later generations. Although many subsequent leaders had *moai* carved for them (often during their lifetimes), their standardization may reflect the idea of an Original Father. Beyond this, why the statues look as they do remains a mystery, as their faces are unlike any depicted in sculpture elsewhere. Perhaps it was just a case of trial and error: one day a carver came up with a face that struck everyone as having exceptional *mana*—so they stuck with it. The faces undeniably possess immense power and gravity.

« None of the statues is known to have had the name of a deity. Instead they were all known by the collective name *aringa ora* (living faces): they are clearly generalized rather than individualized portraits. Captain Cook's party heard the term *ariki* (chief) applied to some, while others had nicknames such as 'Twisted Neck,' 'Tattooed One' and even 'Stinker' (even today, the islanders frequently use nicknames for each other and for visitors.) »

Paul Bahn and John Flenley
Easter Island, Earth Island

The statues may have been positioned by the sea to serve as protection, a spiritual buffer between a frail civilization and the mighty ocean. Tidal waves are known to have wreaked havoc on Rapa Nui, so the need for protection was not imaginary. Mythically the border between sea and land also represents the frontier between life and death, thus guarded by the *moai*. Why then did the statues face inland rather than directing their potent gaze toward the sea? Apparently it was more important that people could see their faces, converse with them, interact with them as living personalities, both in everyday life and special ceremonies; they were an integral part of each settlement. Bahn also points out that, in many societies, the presence of ancestors (their physical remains or images) was regarded as proof that the land belonged to their descendants. This may have been the Easter Islanders' way of "literally staking a claim" to this farflung outpost.

Falling from Grace

The classic *moai* are acknowledged to be one of the great achievements of any Stone Age culture. And they were by no means ancient Rapa Nui's sole accomplishment: its people excelled also in woodworking (such as there was), tattooing, feather art, and *tapa* cloth (made from paper-mulberry and painted in bold designs). Their rock art was extraordinary, and they devised a unique system of language glyphs minutely carved on wooden tablets called *rongorongo*, which still remains largely undeciphered. All in all, the small community on Easter Island left a legacy as rich as any half-dozen Polynesian societies put together.

There are varied ideas about why this was so: Did the island's cooler climate and limited resources serve as a spur to energy and imagination? Were the original immigrants a particularly gifted gene pool? But there are even more ideas about why, after more than a millennium of remarkable peace and productivity, this community self-destructed. The great fall, though a long time in preparing, happened quite quickly. By the time the first Europeans arrived in 1722, the last *moai* was already 75 years old; in the four years between the Spanish visit in 1770 and Cook's in 1774, many of the statues had been overturned and wrecked. There was evidence of violence and strife: large numbers of people hiding in caves, arsenals of clubs and obsidian spearpoints uncovered. It was clear even to those early visitors that some kind of social breakdown had occurred.

Apparently, competition between the island's clan groups had reached a fever pitch by the mid-seventeenth century, climaxing in a legendary battle at Poike (see sidebar, page 49). By this time the Miru clan, claiming direct descent from Hotu Matua, had become by far the most powerful, dominating the culture's economy and religious practice. Through its hereditary chief, the *Ariki henua*, the Miru led the scramble to build the most and the biggest *moai*, as well as demanding tribute in the form of foodstocks and *tapu* fish. Raising sufficient food to nourish an ever-expanding population gradually took a back seat to activities that helped boost a clan's status, like *moai*-building.

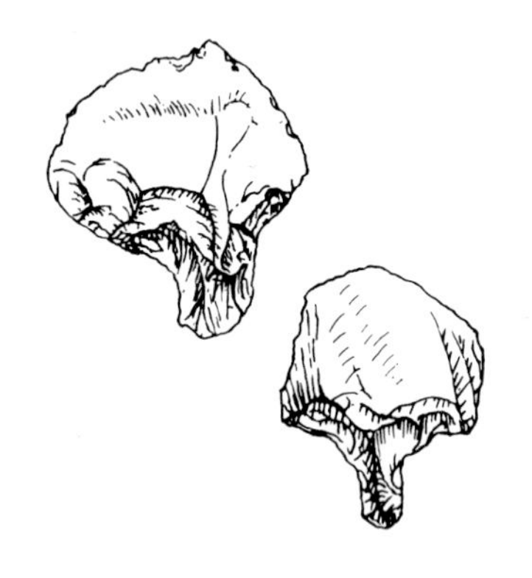

Many factors had a hand in dismantling the island's culture. Feuding and warfare, stealing from family caves, and the proliferation of stone chicken houses to guard this precious food source were symptoms of more subtle and profound changes—most related to environmental degradation. Seabird populations had long since been decimated by uncontrolled egg harvesting; inshore fish and shellfish also were overex-

Above: Drawings of obsidian mataa *found by the 1955 Norwegian expedition; these date from the period of social breakdown. Right: Empty pedestals and the bases of toppled statues at Ahu Vaihu.*

Painted bird symbols in the cave known as Ana Kai Tangata, which translates as "Man Eat Cave"—possibly a reference to cannibalism during times of extreme food shortages.

ploited and grew sparse. One island legend relates that an old woman (possibly a witch) lived in Rano Raraku, and with her breath enabled the statues to move. One day she found the empty shell of a giant lobster and grew so angry at being denied her rightful share that she made all the *moai* fall flat on their faces; they never moved again. This explanation of the statues' toppling, however fanciful, shows the very real link of the social crash to food shortages.

Deforestation of the island had the most far-reaching impact. Large palm trees were once quite abundant, apparently, as well as shrub-sized species used for rope, fuel, carving, and other needs. The islanders had unwittingly hastened the deforestation process by importing Polynesian rats (used for food), which gnawed and destroyed the nuts of the local palm. (They also stole the eggs of ground-nesting birds.) The remaining trees were cut for a variety of purposes—and at a vastly accelerated rate as the *moai*-building became obsessive. Many hundreds were used as rollers and ground to pieces under the transport sledges, if the theory proposing that technology is correct. Not a single palm survived on the

« The toppling was often no mean achievement, and must have involved ropes, levers and a number of men—this may be why Paro, the tallest and heaviest statue ever erected on a platform, was also the last to be overthrown, its huge headdress coming to rest a few metres in front of it. But simple toppling or undermining was often not enough. In many cases, the statues were deliberately beheaded, by placing stones where the fragile neck would fall, for decapitation prevented the statue's re-erection. Most were toppled landward, perhaps to cover the eyes; in one case, a statue resting face-upward had its eye area completely pulverized, again a task of considerable effort. These attacks on head and eyes probably reflect the location of the figures' *mana*—they were not just toppled but had their power totally extinguished. »

Paul Bahn and John Flenley
Easter Island, Earth Island

island by the time of contact; the few hundred growing there today were imported.

As wood grew scarce, the islanders could no longer build canoes large and seaworthy enough to fish far offshore, so they were restricted to the waters close to land—which grew less and less productive. Deforestation also led to increased erosion and impoverishment of the soil.

At the time of the early contacts, Rapa Nui's population was generally estimated to be under 1,000 souls (2,000 may be closer to the real figure), but most recent studies indicate that ancient populations may have reached as high as 6,000 to 8,000, with a decline beginning after around A.D. 1600. If all the agricultural land on the island were put to full production, even higher populations might have been possible—but clearly food production suffered when building *moai* became an all-consuming goal, and when people were fighting each other or hiding out in caves. It's possible, too, that some Malthusian economics were at work: in a totally closed community, the stresses of overpopulation alone could have led to conflicts.

The unraveling of the social fabric led to changes in the island's traditional belief system. The long rule of the ancestors was supplanted around the late 1600s by reverence for a fierce creator god called Make-Make (also known in the Marquesas). Important rituals came to center around fertility symbols: the annual Birdman race for the precious eggs, and celebrations of female sexuality, both depicted in many petroglyphs. The worship of fertility could have contributed further to overpopulation. It's been suggested that the Birdman ritual celebrating the egg was a symbolic attempt to restore this dwindling resource, while actually speeding its decline.

Many have wondered why the Easter Islanders seem never to have ventured off the island in search of other lands and peoples—especially when conditions there grew desperate. The most obvious practical reason is that they no longer had the wood for the large, seagoing canoes that carried other Polynesians hither and yon; probably their canoe-

The Battle at Poike Ditch

Skull found in a lava-tube cave used as a burial site, near Anakena.

The Poike peninsula, a grassy, cliff-girded highland that forms the northeast corner of Rapa Nui, is geologically the oldest part of the island. Its most distinctive feature is a series of elongated trenches, known as the "Poike Ditch," that bisects the neck of the peninsula. Once thought to be a natural feature, it is actually manmade or at least modified by humans, according to researchers.

Legend has it that during the height of civil strife, around the late 1600s, a great battle was fought there between the Hanau Eepe and the Hanau Momoko (the "stocky" versus the "slender" people, or the Long Ears and Short Ears). Versions of the story differ: the most popular recounts that the Hanau Eepe built a huge pyre in the ditch to hold off their enemies, but were surrounded by the Hanau Momoko and driven into their own flames—thus the local name given to the ditch, "The Earth Oven of the Hanau Eepe."

Although Thor Heyerdahl came to believe this story after excavating charcoal remains from the ditch, there is no real proof that a battle took place here. The burned wood could have been from land cleared for farming; others suggest that the ditch was a giant oven used to cook food for quarry workers at nearby Rano Raraku.

Oral traditions further claim that the only "Long Ear" to survive the battle was named Ororoine, and he lived to bear descendants; some modern islanders claim ancestry from him. Ororoine was resurrected for the film *Rapa Nui* in the character of Noro, and the film uses the Poike battle as the climax to its story.

building skills grew rusty as well. There were also long-standing beliefs, going back to Hotu Matua, that the rest of the world had sunk beneath the waves in the cataclysm that forced the original emigration to Rapa Nui; so what was the point of leaving?

Still, it's not hard to imagine a restless young man, with small hope of a decent future, looking out to sea, dreaming of escape, and possibly attempting it in whatever kind of vessel he could patch together. The makers of the film *Rapa Nui* have imagined just such a scenario. In this context, the symbolic depiction of birds and birdmen all over the island takes on new meaning. As Bahn and Flenley point out, they could "fly wherever they liked and hence leave the island, unlike the natives… birds always occupy a prominent place in Oceanic mythology; they

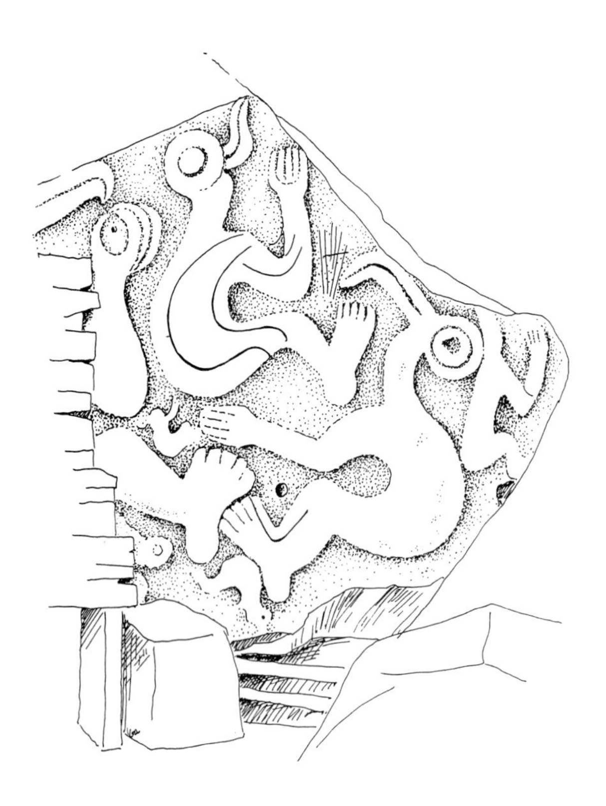

were often thought to have a mystical relationship with the gods, acting as messengers or as transporters of souls...."

And so we come in the film to the young man Noro, gazing thoughtfully at the seabirds circling and crying overhead, and wondering aloud, "Where do you come from? Where do you go?..."

From Contact to Commerce

After the peaceful visit by the French under La Pérouse in 1786, contact between Rapa Nui and the outside world turned violent. As Paul Theroux notes: "The history of Easter Island in the nineteenth century is a long sad story of foreign raiding parties (mainly American and Spanish), of slavery and plunder, leading to famine, venereal disease, smallpox outbreaks, and ultimately the ruin of the culture...."

Above: Drawing by Georgia Lee of birdman petroglyphs at Orongo. Below: Inside one of the caves on Motu Nui is this red-painted bas-relief carving of the god Make-Make.

The first slave raid, in 1805, was led by the American captain of the schooner *Nancy*, out of New London. After a short battle, he managed to capture twelve men and ten women, intending to bring them to the Chilean island Más Afuera to work at a seal-hunting colony there.

Three days after leaving Easter Island, the prisoners' chains were removed, and the men promptly leaped overboard and swam toward the island. They perished, of course.

In succeeding years, other ships were prevented from landing by the islanders' understandable hostility, but they could not hold off the inevitable. Whaling ships stopped at the island to capture women for sexual use, though many no doubt were hidden in the caves. Men from a Russian ship forced their way ashore and managed to trade for a few vegetables. Not all the encounters were hostile, but when the first known missionary set out for Easter Island from Polynesia in 1843, he was never heard from again.

The biggest blow to the island's surviving population came in 1862, when several Peruvian ships gathered in Hanga Roa's harbor and captured several hundred people, destined for slave labor at guano islands off the coast of Peru. After a strong protest by the Catholic bishop of Tahiti, some of these were repatriated; however, most died of smallpox on the voyage home, and the remaining handful brought the epidemic with them to the island. By the mid-1870s, the population had fallen as low as 111.

Missionaries eventually gained a permanent foothold on the island, and have been among its notable personages ever since. They succeeded in converting the islanders to Catholicism, at least on the surface, and the church became a social center of the island. They were also responsible for destroying some "heathen" artifacts, but they did preserve most of the surviving *rongorongo* tablets, and can be credited for their efforts to improve the islanders' material well-being.

Rapa Nui's Secret Script

In 1864, the missionary brother Eugene Eyraud made a discovery that seized the world's imagination almost as much as the *moai*: "In all their houses one can find tablets of wood or sticks with many kinds of hieroglyphic signs. . . ." These tablets were called *rongorongo*, or in their full name *Kohau motu mo rongorongo*—"lines of inscription for recitation." Eyraud thought them the work of the devil and ordered them destroyed, but the Bishop of Tahiti recognized their unique importance as "the first trace of script which has been found in all the islands of Oceania."

Though legends claim that Hotu Matua brought inscribed tablets to the island with him, most experts believe that the practice of carving glyphs on wood did not begin until after the Spanish visit of 1770—when the islanders were asked to put their marks on a document of annexation. The sequence of development isn't clear: they seem to have had glyphs before then, but not the idea of inscribing them in straight, closely spaced rows like the Europeans' writing.

The symbols—some 120 different motifs—are carved in rows of which every other is upside down, so the board was ritually turned during recitations. Although no real translation exists, the glyphs seem to represent whole ideas or phrases rather than syllables or letters. The last islanders truly familiar with their meaning were killed or abducted during the Peruvian slave raids of 1862. The *rongorongo* tablets themselves were mostly burned or hidden during the civil wars; only 29 are known to survive in the world's museums. Some may still rest in the island's secret caves—*tapu* emblems of an old religion thus forever safeguarded from new beliefs.

The Peruvian claim to Easter Island, dating back to 1770, was never pursued (other than by slave raiding), and no other nation laid claim to the island for more than a century. An energetic half-Tahitian shepherd named Alexander Salmon, who came to the island as the representative of a wealthy sheep rancher, tried to make a case for incorporating it into French Polynesia but nothing came of this. Finally, in 1888 the Chilean captain Policarpo Toro formally annexed the island for his country, which has controlled it ever since. Early attempts to establish a Chilean colony failed, but since 1914 there has been an official Chilean presence on Easter Island.

Below: One of Rapa Nui's many carvers working at his craft. Facing page: Film extras recreate a scene of islanders gathering totora *reeds from the crater lake in Rano Raraku, to weave into rafts or house coverings.*

Almost the first thing the Chilean government did after taking possession was to lease virtually the entire island to a British sheep-ranching operation based in Valparaiso. Ostensibly to guard against poaching, they herded all the islanders into the village of Hanga Roa and built a fence around it, declaring the rest of the island off-limits. This could never be fully enforced, however—especially at night, when people would creep out to fish or visit their family caves. The islanders revolted against this oppression in 1914, occasioning the visit of a Chilean warship and more attention from the colonizing power afterwards.

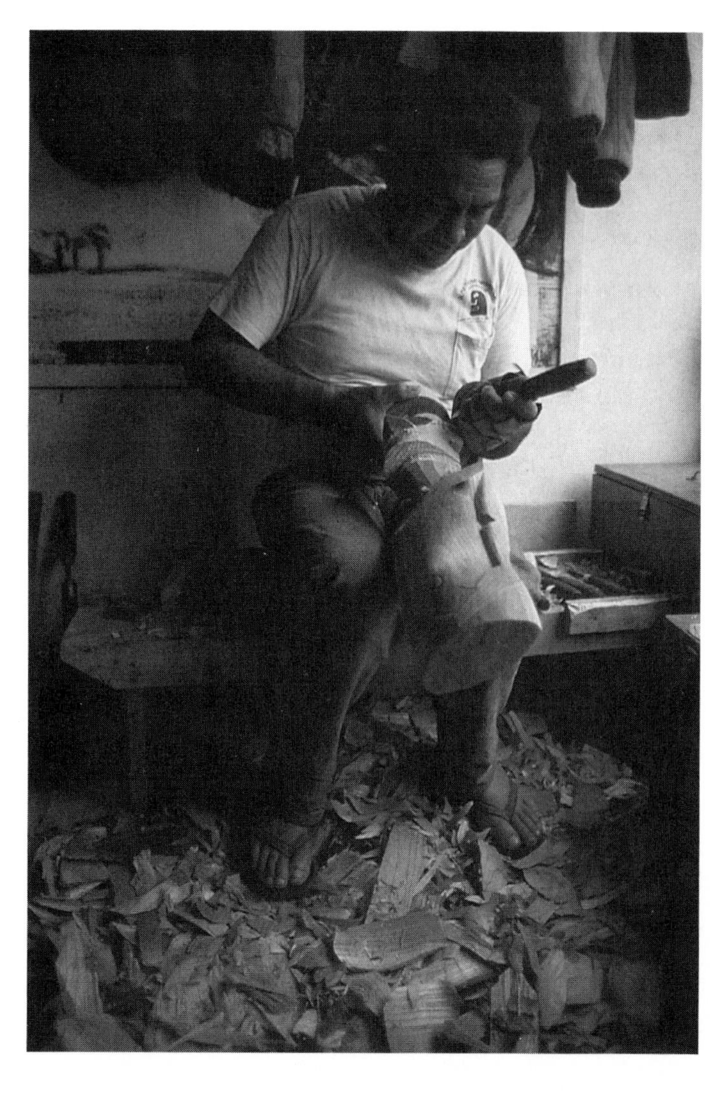

At the time of this event, an English expedition led by a remarkable woman, Mrs. Katherine Routledge, was conducting archeological work on the island. Serious fieldwork had been going on there since a weeklong exploration by a German team in 1882, and the most thorough studies to date had been made by an American group from the *USS Mohican*, led by paymaster William Thompson, in 1886. These early groups did prodigious work in excavating, cataloguing, and mapping the *ahu*, *moai*, and other artifacts, but far more remained for modern-day scientists to investigate. Thor Heyerdahl's 1955 Norwegian expedition opened the current era of intensive research on Rapa Nui, and while his preoccupations led in some bizarre directions, his team accomplished a great deal—including some groundbreaking experiments in how the *moai* were quarried, moved, and erected. Specialists in many

fields of archeology and anthropology continue to make new discoveries.

Today about 2,100 people inhabit Easter Island—a mixed population descended from the original settlers, with infusions of new blood from marriages to South Americans, Polynesians, and others. Regular air service brought vastly increased accessibility, and tourism has become central to the island's economy, including the sale of small woodcarvings, cloth paintings, and rubbings. The ancient tradition of skilled carving remains very much alive on Rapa Nui. "Almost everyone on the island is a sculptor," observed a production artist from the *Rapa Nui* film crew. Other ancestral traditions of ritual and dance have been revived—partly for the benefit of tourists—but they also express the islanders' renewed pride in their extraordinary heritage.

In 1914 the Rapanui rebelled against their confinement by British leaseholders, and sent the company manager this "declaration of war":

June 30, 1914

Now I declare to you, by-and-by we declare to you, which is the word we speak to-day, but we desire to take all the animals in the camp and all our possessions in your hands, now, for you know that all the animals and farm in the camp belong to us, our Bishop Tepano [Jaussen] gave to us originally. He gave it to us in truth and justice. There is another thing, the few animals which are in front of you, are for you to eat. There is also another thing, to-morrow we are going out into the camp to fetch some animals for a banquet. God for us, His truth and justice...

Your friend Daniel Antonio Hangaroa

The island has its problems, certainly. Like many indigenous societies in transition, it suffers from a high rate of alcohol abuse and the desire of young people to emigrate—a much simpler task today! But by all accounts, twentieth-century complications have not destroyed its essential, mysterious allure.

As a recent visitor, Paul Theroux, says, "You come to a place you have read about your whole life, that is part of the world's mythology of mystery and beauty, and somehow you expect it to be overrun—full of signs and guidebooks and brochures, and other similarly rapt pilgrims.... But Easter Island is still itself, a barren rock in the middle of nowhere, littered with hundreds of masterpieces of stone carving, blown by the wind, covered in grass, and haunted by the lonely cries of seabirds."

Editor's Note:

The primary and indispensable source of information and quoted material for Part One is *Easter Island, Earth Island*, by Paul Bahn and John Flenley (Thames and Hudson, 1992). Other sources include *The Happy Isles of Oceania: Paddling the Pacific*, by Paul Theroux; Thor Heyerdahl's *Aku-Aku* and *Easter Island: The Mystery Solved*, and *The Ascent of Man*, by Jacob Bronowski.

« The critical question about these statues is, Why were they all made *alike*? You see them sitting there, like Diogenes in their barrels, looking at the sky with empty eye-sockets, and watching the sun and the stars go overhead without ever trying to understand them. When the Dutch discovered this island on Easter Sunday in 1722, they said that it had the makings of an earthly paradise. But it did not. An earthly paradise is not made by this empty repetition, like a caged animal going round and round, and making always the same thing. These frozen faces, these frozen frames in a film that is running down, mark a civilisation which failed to take the first step on the ascent of rational knowledge. That is the failure of the New World cultures, dying in their own symbolic Ice Age. »

Jacob Bronowski
The Ascent of Man

Facing page: Off Rapa Nui's southwestern cape lie the surf-battered islets of Moto Iti (the pinnacle) and Motu Nui, larger and more distant, which figure in the Birdman competition.

Part Two

RAPA NUI: THE STORY ON FILM

Prologue
A.D. 690

In an aerial shot we see a forest isolated in the vast ocean far below—a tilted triangle of dark green in a white necklace of surf. Crater lakes, like great eyes in deep sockets, stare back up at the sky. The verdant forest is lush, smothering the island above the steep, rocky coast. It's twilight...the sky orange in the west...the moon rising in the east. The camera comes down to earth as the sky darkens. We see low huts, canoes on a silver beach. Planting fields cut like a series of bites into the towering palm forest.

Heavy surf at sunrise looking toward Poike from the island's north coast.

RAPA NUI COAST, NEAR ANAKENA BAY

About two dozen Polynesian settlers huddle around a fire, their backs to the lonely surf.

VOICE (V.O.)
Hotu Matua, you guided us here. What shall we do when you're gone? Should we leave?

The words are addressed to a revered old man lying in their midst. Staring upward. Preparing for death.

HOTU MATUA
No...we searched the ocean for a hundred days before we found this last earth, this navel of the world. There's no way back...

There's an awful silence. The faces hovering over him are downcast.

HOTU MATUA
You can live here. We know that now. There's wood, water, soil for planting and fish in the sea.

One of the hovering faces indicates a small stone likeness of Hotu Matua standing within the dying man's reach.

FACE
Please, leave us your *mana*—your power. We're so few and so alone.

The old man sees their anguish, reaches to touch the little stone carving with a trembling hand. He manages a reassuring smile.

HOTU MATUA
Where I go now you can't follow. But we'll be together again someday ...in the Spiritland...as surely as the sunbirds nest in the cliffs each spring.

FACE
Will you come back for us?

HOTU MATUA
...as surely as the birds...a white canoe?...

He's fading now, seeing things.

FACE
What should we do until then?

On the brink of immortality, the old man stares at the stars defining themselves in the darkening sky overhead.

HOTU MATUA
Remember me.

His eyes close forever. Now a terrible wailing rises from the huddled settlers as they rock and moan their grief. Two of the mourners tear out their earrings and throw them into the fire, a symbol of their loss.

SECOND FACE
Your tears won't bring him back. He's gone now and the old ways with him. We have to think of ourselves now.

We move in on the sightless coral eyes of the little stone statue, then cut to a long shot of the verdant island. The lonely speck of firelight. A spaceship lost in a watery universe.

Fade to black. A legend appears on the screen:

"More than a thousand years later, on Easter Sunday, 1722, a Dutch navigator discovered the most remote inhabited island on the face of the earth and named it...Easter Island.

The dying Hotu Matua bids his followers farewell.

"Twenty-three hundred miles west of Chile and fifteen hundred miles east of Pitcairn Island, the Dutch found a tiny, barren, treeless land inhabited by cannibalistic primitives and gigantic stone statues, remnants of a once flourishing civilization.

"The natives called their island *Te-pito-o-te-Henua*—The Navel of the World—and centuries of total isolation had convinced them the rest of the land had sunk beneath the ocean and they were the only people on earth.

"To this day, no one is completely sure what happened before the Dutch arrived."

[*Readers please note:* The preceding scene, and others included in this published version of the shooting script, were omitted from the final cut of the film released for theatrical viewing.]

Rapa Nui

A.D. 1680

Dawn. As the titles begin to roll, the camera rushes over wavetops from a mile out to sea, headed for an island looming in the cold gray light.

It's a familiar shape, but as we swoop past the rocky islets of Motu Nui and Motu Kao Kao and up the thousand-foot cliff at Orongo, we see there are no more trees, no more forest. Now something else stabs the sky.

Backlit by dawn, three giant stone *moai* (statues), bearing the faintest resemblance to Hotu Matua, stand atop the cliff. The shot moves in on their empty eyes which then become…a wave, rising powerfully in slow motion to cover the sun. It hangs poised for an instant, then crashes into countless bits of frozen spray. At the waterline, wet sand reflects the inexorable sunrise until surf-chased shorebirds blot it away.

RANO RARAKU

Dawn

A *moai* stands in silhouette on the outer slope of the crater called Rano Raraku. In the distance, on the endless ocean horizon, the sun finally breaks free.

A messenger races downslope, past the *moai*; we pan with the running figure to reveal the entire mountainside covered with half-buried, monstrous statues.

Far below on the barren, rocky landscape another statue seems to be inching toward the coast, kicking up dust. Hundreds of antlike figures are moving it. The giant *moai* is fifty feet tall, lashed upright to a log sled, and the antlike figures moving it are men—thin, sweaty Polynesian men—clad in loincloths, their long hair pulled up and tied on their heads in topknots, their faces and bodies covered in elaborate tattoos.

Using ropes and palm log rollers, they slowly force the eyeless monster forward past other, slightly smaller statues strewn beside their path. A team of workers clears large chunks of lava out of the way. Another swarms over the statue, polishing, chipping, finishing the back. Other men heave on ropes. As the sled passes over the log rollers, some hurry to move them from back to front so they can be rolled over again. The faces of the labor gang are not happy.

The log rollers groan and pop from a hundred tons of weight. The gouged track is littered with their smashed predecessors. In the surrounding landscape, a thousand tree stumps tell us where they came from.

The face of the giant is serenely inscrutable and, like all the other *moai*, an abstract echo of the small statue touched by Hotu Matua in the first scene.

Short Ears haul yet another moai *toward the Long Ear village.*

The messenger races past this scene without even giving it a glance. He too is loincloth-clad, tattooed, and topknotted; but, unlike the others, his perforated earlobes are stretched four inches long. He is a Long Ear.

COAST, NEAR THE LONG EAR VILLAGE

Dawn

The rolling grass drops to jagged lava, so the messenger clambers down to the pounding surf. The view shifts to a youth surfing a reed raft against the sunrise, cleaving toward shore. He also has lengthened ears.

MESSENGER

Noro!

Noro finishes the wave goofily, beautifully, prompting nearby applause. Two Long Ear girls shout and giggle from a tidepool. They have tattoos and are bare-breasted, their ears extended with shells. They wear yellow *tapa* cloaks and large woven hats to

Facing page: Noro, wearing ear ornaments and traditional topknot hairstyle, carries a swimming float woven of totora *reeds.*

protect their complexions.

Near the girls, an old Short Ear man and woman crouch on the rocks, checking over their meager catch. They look up at the messenger's slightly disapproving gaze, bow deferentially.

LONG EAR GIRL
That was wonderful, Noro!

He waves back, hurrying out of the water to where the messenger waits.

MESSENGER
The Ariki-mau wants to see you.

Noro clambers up the lava with his raft, and the two boys set off together toward the village.

Back on the *moai* road, the labor gang has moved the giant statue about twenty feet. The two Long Ear youths race past them, Noro shouting hello. In the distance behind the straining Short Ears, the quarry at Rano Raraku sprouts more giant statues and hundreds of working men.

LONG EAR VILLAGE

That morning

From here, on the south coast of the island, you can see from Orongo in the west to the heights of the Poike Peninsula in the east, with nothing but barren, broken plains in between.

The village consists of about forty boat-shaped huts, arrayed in a semicircle facing a central cobbled plaza. Behind the plaza, right above the water's edge, rises the magnificent ceremonial *ahu* platform. Two hundred yards long, built of volcanic stone, it supports eighteen carved *moai*, each at least thirty feet tall. Backs to the sea, coral eyes radiating, they watch over the village, dominating the landscape.

All up and down the stark coast, as far as the eye can see, are more *ahu* and brooding *moai*, and hundreds and hundreds of people. It's a subtle thing, but the Long Ear people seem a bit more well-to-do, a bit more well fed than the Short Ear laborers.

Noro hurries into view, drops his raft, and gives the sacred *moai* a perfunctory bow. He glances at Long Ear women weeping over a *tapa*-wrapped body laid out before the *ahu* and runs to a large circular lodge that's obviously a place of importance. Noro crawls past a guard into the low entrance.

In the dimly lit interior, we see in closeup bone dice tossed on the dirt floor. A long-nailed finger carefully examines them. The finger belongs to Tupa, chief priest of the royal Miru clan. The man he answers to is the Ariki-mau—head chief of the island, direct descendant of Hotu Matua… and Noro's grandfather.

GRANDFATHER
Well?

TUPA
Hard to say.

Grandfather sits on a low dais. He's about sixty, his pale skin carefully tattooed, his ears stretched down to his shoulders. Unlike everyone else, his hair and eyebrows are close-cropped and his fingernails are extremely long, like the pinions of a bird. In another year or two he will be senile.

The Machiavellian Tupa is thin with a hooked nose, a small goatee, and bulbous eyes. Other priests sit in the shadows, holding ceremonial canoe paddles with identical faces carved on the blades.

Grandfather watches with concern while Tupa studies the bone die again.

GRANDFATHER
Tupa, tell me the truth.

TUPA

I would if I could, my Ariki. The signs are neither good nor bad. We should look again later, perhaps.

Grandfather cannot hide his disappointment.

GRANDFATHER

I must know when, Tupa.
(points at bone knuckles)
Try something else. Try the smoke again, I think we were getting somewhere with that.

Tupa smiles sublimely and assents, collecting his die. There is a stir outside as Noro crawls through the low opening. The boy automatically kisses the hem of Grandfather's cloak, then sits back on his heels expectantly.

NORO

Matua Tane.

Grandfather takes a reluctant, solemn breath.

GRANDFATHER

Your cousin Epe has fallen while training for the Birdman competition. That's his body lying before the *ahu*, ...You must take his place.

Noro reacts with amazement, and Grandfather nods.

GRANDFATHER

It's what the signs command—according to Tupa.

Noro throws a glance at the priest, who returns a polite bow.

NORO

But...I'm not worthy...I'm not ready.

GRANDFATHER

I know—but there's no one else. They're all dead or gone...except you.
(formally)
So, Noro, the priests of the Miru clan invite you to compete for...for...?

His mind slips. Tupa leans close.

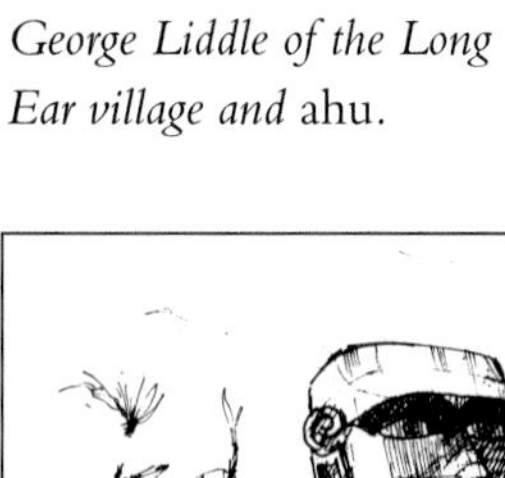

Production drawing by George Liddle of the Long Ear village and ahu.

Tupa, the Miru head priest and Grandfather's trusted counselor, plants an idea in the Ariki-mau's head.

TUPA
The first egg.

GRANDFATHER
...the first egg at Orongo, when Hotu Matua sends his birds in the spring. Will you swim for me—the Ariki-mau—the reigning Birdman?

Noro is nearly too stunned to speak, but stammers his consent. The priests dutifully flutter their paddles and fingernails in not-very-convincing approval. Grandfather addresses them.

GRANDFATHER
Tell the other Long Ears they're wasting their time selecting swimmers because Noro will prevail—making me Birdman for the twentieth year....

His voice becomes edged with bitterness as he stares into the past.

GRANDFATHER
...and erasing the shame of his father ...my son...who swam for me nineteen springs ago.

Noro reddens, drops his eyes. Tupa takes it all in.

GRANDFATHER
We will be restored in the eyes of the Great Parent, Hotu Matua, once again...and he will send the White Canoe at last.

Grandfather lifts Noro's face, beams at him.

Someone else crawls into the lodge now, accompanied by the guard—a dirty, sweaty Short Ear man. It is Heke, a master statue carver, and he prostrates himself before Grandfather, catching his breath.

HEKE
It's finished, Ariki-mau. Will you give your approval?

Grandfather and his entourage prepare to go out and view the new *moai*.

At the edge of the Long Ear village, the giant statue waits on its sled. Around its base, a hundred exhausted Short Ears slump or lie on the ground. Make, a young man of eighteen, stands out from the rest. More frustrated than fatigued, he blows on his rope-burned hands as something offstage brings his people struggling to their feet.

Preceded and flanked by club-wielding *matatoa* (warriors), priests, and various hangers-on, Grandfather is carried on a litter from the village to where the statue waits. The bearers put him down, and Grandfather climbs off, already examining the monster.

This is clearly the biggest, most impressive *moai* anywhere on the coast. Grandfather studies it from every conceivable angle, then casts a hopeful glance out to sea. But the horizon is blank. He sighs.

GRANDFATHER
Nahh... Build another one.

You can almost hear the Short Ears' hearts drop. Even the Long Ears are stunned. Only Tupa smiles. A dozen emotions wash over Heke's numb, dirty face—none of them pleasant. Grandfather pats his shoulder as he heads for the litter.

GRANDFATHER
Heke, take the rest of the day off.

Heke (center), Make, and other Short Ears anxiously await Grandfather's verdict on the new moai.

Attended by other Long Ear chiefs, Grandfather inspects the moai.

Almost beside himself, the old master carver throws himself on the ground in supplication, waves toward the statue.

HEKE
Ariki, please may I ask…

Tupa frowns on such impudence.

HEKE
…how does this *moai* displease the gods?

Not completely sure, Grandfather takes one last look at the looming monster as he's hoisted onto the bearers' shoulders.

GRANDFATHER
It's too small.

And with a jingle of shell necklaces, Grandfather disappears into the village, taking what's left of the Short Ears' spirit with him.

Now Tupa snaps his fingers and indicates the statue. With reluctant but practiced moves, Make and the others chop the ropes binding the sled, allowing the logs to part. Then they heave on the lines around the behemoth's neck. The statue rocks a moment until they find the center of gravity, then all fifty feet of it slowly slams face first into the ground with a quaking thud.

The Short Ears stare at their discarded handiwork in abject disbelief, then start the long trek back to the quarry. Two of them lift Heke from the dust and help him along. Only Make is left, staring darkly after Tupa.

Jason Scott Lee: A Rising Star in Action

As the leading character Noro, 25-year-old Jason Scott Lee carries a big load in *Rapa Nui*: he must not only bring off the action/adventure sequences with panache, but also convincingly portray a boy's passage into manhood and his budding awareness of social injustice.

Playing indigenous people is nothing new to this Hawaiian native, who last year starred as the Eskimo Avik in the Cannes-acclaimed film *Map of the Human Heart*, and as Bruce Lee in *Dragon*, the film biography of the martial-arts legend. Recreating Lee's life prepared Jason well for the physical demands of *Rapa Nui*. Relying on his natural strength and grace as well as skills in Jeet Kune Do and gymnastics, he did much of his own stunt work, including diving off high rocks and swimming in treacherous waters.

Jason appreciates the opportunity the film gave him and other Polynesian actors to showcase themselves in traditional roles. Before getting the call to audition for Noro, he had been involved in dramatic readings of Polynesian creation myths. Raised in Hawaii in a similar kind of Polynesian atmosphere, he could adapt more easily than some in the cast and crew to the playful, relaxed culture on Rapa Nui. "It's been incredible to live among these people," he says, "and see the uncorrupted spirit the children carry."

Director Kevin Reynolds says of Jason, "Some people just have a charisma that the camera likes, and he's got it. It's a gift; it's not something you can learn. And you need that in your lead for any picture."

The High Priest, disappearing into the dust cloud thrown up by the fallen *moai*, is startled by a strange sight coming the other way. Noro marches out of the dust, imitating Tupa and the warriors, hiding something under his cloak. Trying to keep a rigidly straight face, he stomps straight up to Make and strikes a fists-on-hips pose à la Yul Brynner.

MAKE

What are you supposed to be?

NORO

(mock sternly)

Are you blind, Short Ear? You address the Birdman.

And with a giddy whoop, he reaches under his cloak and tosses a pair of squawking chickens at Make, then leaps in the air and starts running circles around him like some Polynesian Daffy Duck. He gooses Make with one of the chickens and finally gets the response he wants. Make starts chasing him. Around and around they go, scrambling over the fallen *moai*, Noro whooping deliriously. His playfulness is infectious and despite himself, Make breaks into a smile.

MAKE

Bird*woman* is more like it.

The boys take off across the stumped landscape, tossing a squawking chicken like an errant football. Hungry Short Ears snatch up the other bird.

A VOLCANIC HILLSIDE

Sunset

From atop the steep slope of a grassy cinder cone, a strange apparatus rockets toward the camera. It's a banana sled—two banana trees lashed together—piloted by a Long Ear youth. The sled bounces once, twice, is suddenly airborne. The pilot somersaults

Noro and Make play a rough game of tag with a pair of chickens Noro has stolen from Tupa.

violently all the way to the bottom.

On the hilltop, other Long Ear youths laugh hysterically at his crash. As Make and Noro clamber up the slope from the banana grove inside the crater, the next one mounts his sled and gets a starting push. He hurtles down at incredible speed. The sled flips and disintegrates, and the rider wobbles to his feet. Hair askew, scratched to hell, he raises his arms triumphantly.

The next rider does a fifty-yard face plow. The guys up top love it.

NORO

(to Make, giggling)
You first.

MAKE

No, you, Birdboy.

NGAARA

Come on—take your filthy Short Ear and get off the hill.

Noro "flips off" Ngaara, a mean-looking youth, and mounts his sled with the chicken.

NORO

We go together, then.

Make mounts too, trying to ignore the Long Ears' sneers. At Noro's signal, they give him a shove. Make pushes off by himself. Whooping, hair flying, Noro manages to hang on almost all the way.

The wild ride makes Make laugh and forget his cares. For a brief moment, he's free. Lying flat on his back, he holds on longer than anyone, until his sled hits a hidden rock and stops. Make keeps going, sliding inches past where Noro lies crashed.

NORO

(groaning)
I won.

The banana slide: Noro and Make race down the slope.

Make points to the chicken squawking at their feet.

MAKE
The chicken won.

NORO
You can keep it—second prize.

MAKE
What's first?

Noro, remembering something, turns away and glances at the sinking sun. He scrambles to his feet and takes off with a wave. Left holding the chicken, Make watches Noro disappear. His glee fades as reality crashes back. He looks down at himself, wonders what he thought he was happy about.

RANO RARAKU QUARRY
Night

Close shot on an earth oven—a fire pit lined with rocks. A stick pokes at a few *kumara* (sweet potatoes) roasting in the coals. We're in the middle of the Short Ear camp. They live where they work in the quarry at Rano Raraku, on the outer slope of the crater amidst the giant statues. Numerous fires illuminate the scene, casting fantastic *moai* shadows.

There's not much to eat here—just potatoes and sugar cane. The abundant things are exhaustion, despair…and kids, hundreds of them. Far too many mouths. And yet these people are singing and dancing around one particularly big fire in their equivalent of The Blues. Young women writhe to the sensuous beat.

Among them is Ramana, a Short Ear beauty, dark and lean with lovely eyes and mouth. Her dancing is discreet but heartfelt. One look at her face and you'd trust anything she says. You would also see sadness and a fear to hope.

A figure moves in the darkness on the edge of camp, slipping from statue to statue. Ramana sees Noro beyond the other faces. She quietly leaves the dancing as the Short Ears exchange knowing looks and frowns.

Ramana moves among the giants, searching for her lover. From out of nowhere, Noro grabs her and pulls her into the night.

Just after they have left, Make appears in camp, hiding the precious chicken under a tapa cloak. He searches for Ramana, asking everyone he can collar where she is. Finally one woman confirms his suspicions, and Make storms off, throwing the chicken over his shoulder as many hands grab for it frantically.

HEADLAND AT TEREVAKA

Dawn

The sun comes up over a stunning view. High above the sweeping, treeless landscape, the lovers lie on a bed of matted grass. Ramana measures something in the sky with her hands.

RAMANA

...and when the morning star is two hands above the horizon in midsummer, that's due west.

NORO

And they could read the currents far out at sea?

RAMANA

Yes. They'd strip off, then jump in the water...

(grins)

The Short Ear camp in Rano Raraku at night, as cooking fires illuminate the moai.

Noro and Ramana seal their bond.

...and feel it with their skin.

Noro is disbelieving.

RAMANA
My father is descended from the navigator on Hotu Matua's canoe. He should know.

NORO
How come no one else knows this?

RAMANA
It's not important to them anymore.

Noro marvels at her.

NORO
Marry me.

She laughs and rolls on her back, then searches his eyes for something false, some sign of a joke...but doesn't see it. Finds another reason to doubt.

RAMANA
They'll never allow it.

NORO
Grandfather has to give me something if I swim for him.

She still doubts, saying that she's accused of wanting Noro only because he's a Long Ear. She wonders if he only wants her for pleasure, but he insists he intends to marry her.

They resume lovemaking. She asks a final question.

RAMANA
Have you told Make?

After a beat, he responds.

NORO
Not yet.

SHORT EAR CAMP

Dawn

Make sleeps under a crude palm frond shelter, curled up against the cold. The camp coughs and stirs, revealing its smoky squalor in the growing light.

New figures emerge from the morning mist, waking the dozing

Short Ears. Tupa and his priests march wordlessly to the vast quarry wall. Tupa examines the rock, takes a block of chalk from an assistant, and begins to scratch an outline in great arcing sweeps on the surface of the wall. He walks on and on, dragging the chalk above his head, as the Short Ears watch in disbelief.

The scratching seems endless. When Tupa stops at last, the new *moai* he has outlined is enormous, gargantuan—almost twice as large as the last one. He looks at Heke's stunned face and finally speaks.

TUPA
You have six moons.

The Short Ears gasp and fume.

HEKE
Priest, that's impossible. The last *moai* took six moons and it wasn't half as big.

TUPA
Stop work on all the other *moai*. Focus only on this one.

HEKE
Yes, but even then—

TUPA
Should I find another master carver?

Heke swallows, fights his overpowering fatigue, manages to pull himself erect.

HEKE
No, I am the best.

TUPA
The Ariki wants it finished before the Birdman competition in the spring.

Tupa accuses the old fisherman and his wife of breaking a tapu.

Getting Inside the Ariki-mau

In the complex and challenging role of Noro's grandfather, the chief of Rapa Nui's reigning Miru clan, Eru Potaka-Dewes makes a memorable impression. A Maori from New Zealand, Eru came to acting after working for 25 years as an Anglican minister. Much of that time he spent as chaplain in a mental institution, which he thinks gave him some insight into his character's progressive dementia and his delusions of a white canoe as salvation.

Director Kevin Reynolds was worried that they would have trouble finding an actor who could capture the delicate balance of Grandfather's behavior. "Here's a guy who at one time was probably a pretty capable leader, but who's now so far removed from reality, by his dementia and his own choosing, that he's got a kind of otherworldly, almost comic quality about him. And I didn't think we'd find anyone who could pull it off. But since the beginning of the picture, Eru has become the character more and more. He *is* Grandfather."

Eru, who has appeared previously in Patricia Grace's film *Eels* and in *The Piano*, believes that everyone has some sort of white canoe—a great goal in his or her life. For him, it would be to bring international focus to Polynesia's indigenous people. He sees *Rapa Nui* as one way to promote this goal, and to strengthen ties between its people and his own.

About to depart, Tupa spots spots the old fisherman and his wife from the opening scene, limping into camp with their morning catch. He inspects the fish, finding one that is *tapu*—forbidden to all but the Ariki-mau at this time of year. Although the old couple protests that they would never break a *tapu* and were planning to bring the fish to the Ariki-mau, Tupa kills the fisherman with a vicious stroke of his heavy ceremonial paddle. He sweeps off with the fish.

As the shattered people digest what's happened, Ramana walks back into camp, halting in shock at the sight of the fisherman's body and his weeping, broken wife. Hard looks are thrown her way. Someone spits. Seeking an explanation, she makes eye contact with Make. He's a caul-dron of anger, disappointment, and hurt. Ramana breaks his gaze, hurries away.

LONG EAR VILLAGE

Day

Before a considerable crowd, a priest conducts a preliminary rite of the Birdman ritual, summoning the Long Ear clans to announce their competitors.

Noro impatiently goes through his part in this event, waiting for a chance to tell Grandfather of his plans.

Noro finally gets Grandfather's attention. After getting rid of the nosy Tupa, he cautiously broaches the subject: He'd like to to get married after the Birdman contest. Grandfather is delighted with this idea, and teases Noro about which of the sexy Long Ear girls he's chosen. Then Noro drops his bombshell.

Grandfather reacts to Noro's news that he wants to marry a Short Ear.

NORO

She's Short Ear...That's why I need your permission.

Grandfather looks like he's been slapped. He orders the litters bearers to put him down. They do so, and back away from his brewing wrath.

GRANDFATHER

Are you turning out like your father? Are you trying to provoke the gods as he did?

Noro denies it in vain.

GRANDFATHER

Here I am giving you a chance to make up for what he did, and now you're acting exactly like him!

This strikes a bitterly deep nerve in Noro.

NORO

I'm *not* like him, Grandfather! You know that. I would never dishonor you or the gods.

GRANDFATHER

Then what is this talk? A *Short Ear*?!

Stung, Noro raises his head.

NORO

Do you want me not to swim for you?

The old man considers this for a moment, seems to soften a bit.

GRANDFATHER

No—the bones say it has to be you. No one else can atone for your

« One day Father Sebastian came to take us with him to Ana o Keke, the holy bleaching place of the *neru* virgins. *Neru* was the name given to specially chosen young maidens who in old days were confined in a deep cave to become as pale and white as possible for special religious festivals when they were to be shown to the public. For a long, long time they might see neither the light of day nor other people, and their food was carried to the cave and pushed through the opening by women appointed for the purpose. The natives could still remember that when the smallpox epidemic raged all over the island after the slaves returned from the mainland, it did not reach the *neru* maidens, but they died of starvation in their cave because there was no longer anyone to bring them food. »

Thor Heyerdahl
Aku-Aku: The Secret of Easter Island

father's sin. That's why the White Canoe hasn't been sent. After nineteen springs—nineteen winners—what else could it possibly be? Except the statues.

He demands to know the name of Noro's choice.

GRANDFATHER
Haoa's daughter? Haoa the canoe builder? The one I banished?

NORO
Yes.

Grandfather rolls his eyes in disgust.

GRANDFATHER
He's the one who trained your father for the Birdman race! He's the one who put all those stupid ideas in your father's...father's...

NORO
...head?

GRANDFATHER
(more confidentially)
Why do you have to marry this girl? Can't you just take her and be done with it?

NORO
I love her, Grandfather. Weren't you ever in love?

A beat. The old man sighs resignedly.

GRANDFATHER
All right. Let me talk to the priest.

Before Noro can stop him, Grandfather has walked over to Tupa and begun explaining Noro's request. Tupa listens, head tilting curiously, eyes drilling Noro, lips set in a Mandarin smile.

After conferring, they inform Noro that there's only one way he can marry Ramana without provoking the wrath of the gods: She must consent to be imprisoned in the Cave of the White Virgins to be "purified"—her skin bleached paler—for the entire six months until the Birdman race. Noro angrily refuses to demand such a sacrifice, but Grandfather won't budge—he can't risk Hotu Matua's displeasure.

GRANDFATHER
Good, then it's settled. You know what I'm thinking, Tupa, while we've been standing here?...Didn't the old stories say Hotu Matua wore a hat?

RANO RARAKU QUARRY
Day

A stone pick strikes the quarry wall, throwing off sparks and dust. All along the outline drawn by Tupa, dozens of Short Ears are hard at work, hammering away. Heke has just received new instructions from a Long Ear priest, and can't believe what he's heard.

HEKE

Hats?!

PRIEST

Yes, and they must be red—the royal color—and we want them immediately...

Noro makes his way through this industrious scene, through legions of laborers making picks and carting away debris, past a line of workers bearing cut *totora* reeds and calabashes of water to soften the stone. He greets those he knows, and continues downslope, entering the wide, shallow bowl where more statues stand half-finished. The whole place is charred black by fires set to burn off grassy stubble for planting. There aren't many planters or plants.

Making his way down to the shallow lake at the bottom of the crater, he finds Ramana in the midst of a mob of shrieking Short Ear girls who are tormenting her, ducking her head underwater, pulling her hair, and pelting her with insults for daring to choose a lover outside her class.

They break off when Noro appears, and he and Ramana flee to an old favorite refuge: the palm grove on the slopes of Terevaka. It's the last remaining grove of trees on the island. Stretching all around them is a grassland full of palm stumps.

The lovers thread their way toward the center of the grove, to a giant palm that bears their name symbols carved in the trunk. They slouch against the tree's base, fingering the

Short Ear girls torment Ramana for daring to love a Long Ear.

Right: Under their special tree, Ramana tells Noro she will submit to the test of the Virgin Cave. Facing page: Ramana is lowered down the cliffside toward the cave entrance.

carved glyphs—exact replicas of smaller ones tattooed on their shoulders. Ramana can't contain her excitement.

RAMANA
He said no, didn't he? Well?

NORO
Actually, he said yes.

Ramana lights up.

NORO
If I win... and *if* you stay in the Virgin Cave until the race.

Her face falls. She turns away. Noro tries to downplay the issue.

NORO
I said no... It doesn't matter—we'll just go on the way we have. We don't have to live Long Ear or Short Ear. We'll just keep to ourselves and—

RAMANA
I'll do it.

NORO
(gently)
Ramana, it's completely dark in that cave. You can't stand up. You can hardly move. You—

She whirls to him, eyes wild with excitement and purpose.

RAMANA
I'll *do* it... if you'll swim. If this is my only chance to have you, I'll take it. I don't want to be secret or forbidden anymore. They think we don't love each other enough to go through with this, but they're wrong—about me.

She searches his eyes. In the background, another tree falls.

THE VIRGIN CAVE

Sunset

The setting sun lights coastal rocks covered with petroglyphs of female vulvas. The camera tilts up from the petroglyphs along a beautiful bare leg to find Ramana, standing with feet

spread on two elaborately carved boulders.

Tupa and a couple of other priests step forward to examine her private parts. Noro watches with concern from nearby. After a moment of probing, Tupa gives Ramana a dry, knowing look.

Now Ramana steps down, crossing to a large reed basket at the edge of the cliff. She is helped in, and the basket is swung over the side by a crude crane. As Ramana is lowered down the sheer face, Noro moves to where he can see her descent.

Far below, yet still hundreds of feet above the crashing waves, two priests reel Ramana in to a precarious perch. She climbs out of the basket and immediately sees the small black mouth of the Virgin Cave. The priests start to guide her inside.

RAMANA

Wait...

She turns, watches the last trace of sun vanish into the sea. Now she looks up at Noro and waves. With a last look, they fix each other in their minds. Then Ramana swallows and nods to the priests, who help her squirm backwards into the little cave. When she disappears, they cross the entrance with *tapa* strips and seal it with wet ochre. Then they climb into the basket and are hoisted away.

Tupa approaches Noro, oozing sincerity.

TUPA

I'm sure her skin will grow as pure as a baby's...but I doubt if her virginity will. It'll be our little secret.

The Girl in the Cave

Undoubtedly one of the toughest roles in *Rapa Nui* is that of the "trophy bride" Ramana, who sacrifices herself to prove her love and conceives a child that carries the future of a culture. After a long search, the producers chose Sandrine Holt, a young actress from Toronto whose exotic Eurasian looks are matched by a haunting screen presence.

"Sandrine is obviously gorgeous, and you can understand why the guys would be vying for her," says Kevin Reynolds. "She also brings a mysteriousness to the character—you're not always sure what's going on back there. In the script it's described as a sadness that's afraid to hope."

Written into the part is the need to balance Ramana's physical appeal with her inner strength. It's she who carries the legacy, through her father, of the Polynesian navigators who discovered Rapa Nui, and who convinces Noro that her ordeal in the Virgin Cave is their only hope for marriage. For a young actress far from home, the role also brought some real-life isolation. Since her scenes come early and late in the film and not all were shot at once, she had to spend many empty hours on the island while others went on working—the equivalent of Ramana's exile in the cave.

In 1991, Sandrine was honored with a Canadian "Genie" nomination for Best Supporting Actress for her portrayal of Annuka, the Algonquin girl in Bruce Beresford's saga *Black Robe*. For that role, she spent three months shooting in the winterbound forests of northern Quebec—good preparation for the challenges of *Rapa Nui*.

RANO RARAKU QUARRY

Night

It's the end of the working day. A last few weary carvers climb down from the scaffolding and make their way over to where everyone hungrily waits for the Long Ear overseer to distribute food. He and his assistants pull scrawny-looking *kumaras* from their baskets and put one in each pair of outstretched hands.

The food ration has been cut—again. Over the Short Ears' protests, the overseer explains that the crops have gotten smaller. He suggests that they'd have more to eat if they didn't have so many babies, further angering the Short Ears.

The overseer's assistant brandishes a club to reinforce his authority. After a moment, a quiet giant named Atta steps forward and passively puts out his rough hand.

OVERSEER

That's a good lad, Atta. Anyone else?

Make ignores them all, moodily watching his *kumara* roast. Make's *kumara* starts to crawl out of the fire by itself. He looks down, sees the escaping vegetable...and the fish hook that's been used to snag it. He grabs the line and whirls behind the rock it leads to. He raises his figurine to strike the thief. Noro looks up at him.

NORO

(grinning)

Hungry?...Come on.

AROUND THE ISLAND

Night

Noro and Make race across the stark landscape. Noro is playfully competitive; Make is not. There's something aggressive about the way he runs. Suddenly in the darkness they come upon clusters of feathered sticks stuck atop piles of rocks—ominous markers.

Noro and Make race each other around the island.

NORO

Tapu...we're in the Poike.

Noro and Make freeze. Whatever it is, they take it very seriously, honoring this invisible boundary and wheeling the other way. They race on until they reach a grove where palm fronds sway in a moonlit breeze.

NORO

(breathless)

I won.

Make shakes his head testily, doesn't even want to start. Noro uncovers a small earth oven hidden beneath a sheltering tree—the same big palm he and Ramana visited earlier. He pulls out roasted bananas and a whole chicken.

MAKE
Who'd you steal it from?

NORO
(grinning)
Tupa... again.

He tosses half the bird to Make, who feels guilty about this windfall food but ravenously devours it neverthe-less. Noro watches a moment, then hands his friend the other half.

Nostalgically he reaches high up the trunk of the big palm to where older, boyish carvings scar the bark.

NORO
Remember when we were little? You and Ramana and I used to come up here all the time and climb this thing ...back when there were more trees.

MAKE
Things change.

Noro gazes past the thinning palms over the stump-studded landscape, as if noticing it for the first time.

NORO
They say all the land was covered with trees once. I guess Hotu Matua will send for us before they're all gone ...at least that's what Grandfather says.

Make spits out a chicken bone, shakes his head in disgusted amazement.

MAKE
You really believe all that shit.

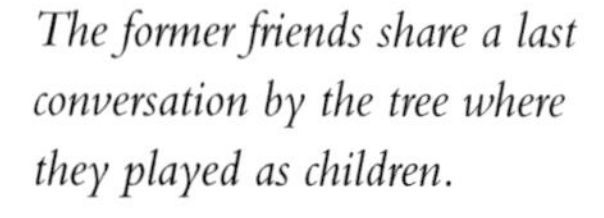

The former friends share a last conversation by the tree where they played as children.

NORO

(surprised)
Don't you?

MAKE

I only believe what I can see and what I can feel...and what I don't have.

He hoists the chicken for emphasis. Make wants to know why Noro sought him out, and Noro tells him he'd welcome some advice about the Birdman race—who are the most dangerous opponents. Make feels no obligation to help him.

MAKE

Why? So your grandfather can stay Birdman another year and work us all to death?

NORO

I got other reasons.

Noro pulls back the foliage at the base of the big palm, revealing his and Ramana's signs.

NORO

They're going to let us marry...if I win. I *have* to win, Make.

Make stares at the lovers' marks, stunned.

MAKE

Where is she?

NORO

The White Virgin cave...until the race.

A dozen emotions swarm over Make's face. He quivers with rage and frustration.

MAKE

You let them put her in that hole?

NORO

She wanted to! It's the only way—otherwise they said the gods would—

MAKE

There are no gods other than the

The Che Guevara of Easter Island

As Make, the dark champion of the Short Ears, Brooklyn native Esai Morales brings a spark of radicalism to the role. Drawing from his own island heritage, Puerto Rico, Esai was intent on capturing the near-indomitable strength of laborers, people who spend their entire lives working with their hands. He chose to meet the physical rigors of *Rapa Nui* by following a regimen of swimming, rock climbing, and stone carving under the guidance of Easter Island expert and former Cousteau diver Henri Garcia.

Esai made his film debut opposite Sean Penn in the 1982 film *Bad Boys*. He has appeared more recently in *Don't Do It* and *Freejack*, but is best known for his role as Richie Valens's brother in the 1987 box-office hit *La Bamba*. Esai has also enjoyed a thriving career in television and stage, and has won the L.A. Critics Drama Award and a New York Image Award. He's been recognized as among the 100 most influential Hispanics by *Hispanic Business* magazine.

"Make's the Che Guevara of Easter Island," Esai asserts. "He's a true socialist for the people. He's got a good heart, a strong heart, and he's fiercely determined. He would actually die for them when no one else would." Esai found great depth and power in his complex character, saying, "To this day I'm still trying to figure him out."

When he wasn't in front of the camera, Esai assisted the director, using his Spanish, film savvy, and passion for the story to help motivate the Easter Island extras in the crowd scenes. "I wanted to give them emotional stimulus as opposed to technical stimulus." The experience will surely serve Esai well in his next ambition: to direct.

ones we make up! There's no "Spirit-land!" There's no Hotu Matua coming back for us! There's nothing out there but water! This…
(stabs a finger at the ground)
…is all there's ever been or ever will be—no matter how many idiot statues we build!

The palms sigh overhead as Noro stares at him, finally comprehending.

NORO
You love her too…that's it, isn't it?

Make throws the rest of the chicken carcass at Noro's feet and suddenly stands.

MAKE
I don't need your little Long Ear handouts anymore.

He stalks away, pausing by the big tree.

MAKE
And we were never friends.

ORONGO
Day

Alone, Noro walks the windswept, knife-edged ridge of Rano Kau crater and looks down at the route he must take as a Birdman competitor. The drop is sheer, the footing treacherous.

A mile away, Motu Nui waits. Noro swallows, turns away. He walks along the coast toward Haoa's cave—a huge lava tube that opens up directly onto the sea. It's a dramatic, lonely place.

In the yawning entrance lie the bodies of several canoes—some smashed, some in pieces, some that have been patched many times. There's not a whole canoe in sight. Noro looks around at the tools of a canoemaker's trade—obsidian blades, stone hammers and adzes—and calls into the darkness.

NORO
Haoa?

Quietly a big man appears out of the shadows.

NORO
Haoa, will you train me to compete for the Birdman?

Haoa looks him up and down.

HAOA
My daughter sits in a cave because of you.

NORO
I'd like to make it worth her while.

High on the crater edge of Rano Kau, Noro scouts the route of the Birdman race.

They say you know the cliffs and currents better than anyone...And you trained my father.

Haoa remembers.

HAOA

The crazy Long Ear.

NORO

He won.

HAOA

Yes, he did. Then one day he climbed in a canoe—one of *my* canoes—sailed over the horizon and never came back. Got me banished to this place.

Noro insists he's not like his father and offers to pay whatever Haoa asks for his coaching.

HAOA

Will you? Then make the forests grow back so I have wood to work.

He indicates his patchwork canoes.

HAOA

...and explain to me why Ramana's skin isn't good enough for a Long Ear.

Noro doesn't even try to answer.

NORO
Will you train me?

HAOA
No...You're too ignorant.

Haoa turns back to his work.

COAST NEAR ORONGO
Day

Though a powerful swimmer, Noro flounders in the high surf, trying not to swallow too much water. The big blue swells pick him up and hurl him back toward the jagged rocks no matter how well he strokes. He manages to time an exit and keep from being dashed to bits, but climbs onto the rocks completely spent and shivering. Catching his breath, he looks across the churning inlet, up the short cliff on the other side.

A pathetic figure—the recently widowed Short Ear fisherwoman—stumbles along the cliff edge looking for food. She comes to a line of feathered sticks stuck in piles of rocks—boundary markers—and turns inland to avoid the *tapu*. On the other side of the line, Long Ears till a meager field...but meager is better than nothing. The starving old woman walks the line, finding a grain now and then but observing the invisible boundary as if it were solid rock.

Watching her, Noro recognizes injustice for the first time.

THE VIRGIN CAVE
Night

Like the mouth of a tomb, the little cave yawns in the dim blue light. The only sound is the mournful wind fluttering the strips of the *tapa* "seal."

Both Make and Noro visit Ramana on this night—her forty-fifth within the cave—as they do frequently, bringing food and trying to give comfort and encouragement. Make still holds hope that she may change her mind; he asks why she can't love someone of her own kind. Ramana reminds him that we can't choose

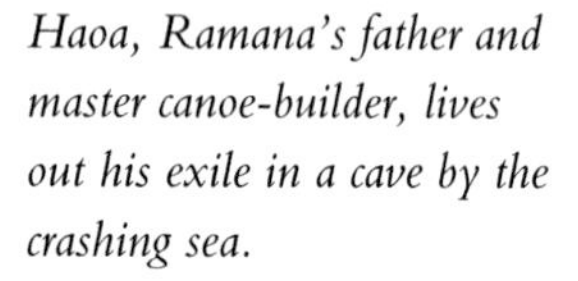
Haoa, Ramana's father and master canoe-builder, lives out his exile in a cave by the crashing sea.

Short Ear workers labor at top speed to finish the Monster moai *by the deadline. One, standing on the statue, carries calabashes of water to soften the stone for carving.*

whom we love—only whose love to accept.

RANO RARAKU QUARRY

Dawn

We pull back across a gray stone shape, revealing the silhouette of lips, chin, nostrils. At first we don't realize the scale until a bowed figure—Heke—climbs an ear and walks along the bridge of the nose out onto the whale-sized torso.

More weary figures now emerge from the quarry camp, dwarfed by the stone giant. We move up in a crane shot to show scaffolding, tons of waste spilling down the hill, and hundreds of laborers struggling to free the impassive monster from the rock. They're already starting on the keel.

Pick...pick...pick...A dozen blows for a millimeter of progress in the dark, cramped space under the figure's back....Up above, Heke shouts orders to masons carving the *moai*'s long, delicate fingers.

Bad news spreads quickly through the camp....

SHORT EARS
They've cut the ration...The ration's been cut!

...from the pick makers to the carvers to the women weaving baskets and hats. Bitterness spreads all the way up the ropes to the top of the quarry.

BETWEEN VILLAGES

Day

Farther down the coast, on a hillside between Rano Raraku and the Long Ear village, a bird swoops right in

« Not much of a mark was made by each blow, hardly more than a gray patch of dust, but with another blow, and one more, and still another, something was gained. And at intervals the men grabbed the calabash and splashed water on the rock face, to soften it where they cut and to prevent splinters from flying in their eyes. »

Thor Heyerdahl
Aku-Aku: The Secret of Easter Island

front of us—actually it's a large kite made of reed and bearing an abstract human face. It steadies for a moment, then swoops again, and we tilt down along the *tapa* string to find…Grandfather, flying the kite, accompanied by his ever-present entourage.

He follows the movements of the kite—yet another sacred oracle—with breathless attention, quizzing Tupa for his interpretation of its erratic darting and plunging.

In the background, a Short Ear labor gang is inexplicably rolling huge plugs of red scoria stone across the landscape, out of frame.

A delegation of Long Ear chiefs interrupts Grandfather and launches into a litany of complaints—about their neighbor Long Ears taking too many fish, about the shortage of wood for canoes (they gesture toward the Short Ears felling still more), about the slowdown in crop production. All agree that their problems can be traced to the Short Ears' having too many children.

Grandfather can't be bothered

with such earthly matters. He turns to board his litter and jumps at the sight of Atta, covered in scoria dust like some red devil. The big man points toward the Long Ear village.

ATTA

Hats.

GRANDFATHER

Hats?... Ah, yes!

He looks off in the distance toward the magnificent row of *moai*. One has a stone ramp built up the back of it. Atop its head sits a carved red scoria hat—the purpose of the rolling plugs.

GRANDFATHER

Mmmmyyyeeaah... I like it. Okay. Much better... I think the ancestors like it too.
(to Atta)
One on each head.

Grandfather is hoisted aboard his litter and moves off.

Tupa lingers for a moment of intrigue with the Long Ear Chiefs, who resent this new mark of distinction reserved for the Miru *moai*. In particular, Tupa must reassure one who aims to become the next Birdman.

FIRST LONG EAR CHIEF

Why would I make you my minister if you can't even control this old fool?

TUPA

I got him to pick the young fool for the race, didn't I? Now your Ngaara will surely win.

HAOA'S CAVE

Twilight

Hidden behind rocks at the base of a cliff, Haoa hauls in an empty fish hook. Huge waves crash and spray him as he crouches, casts the line again. Now another wave thunders beside him—and, unbelievably, hurls someone up onto the rocks.

It's Noro. Coughing and bruised, spitting up water, he finally rolls over and sees Haoa looking at him.

NORO

I'm training.

Now his gaze drifts to three small fish lying by Haoa's feet.

HAOA

(a disgusted monotone)
Oh, forgive me, Ariki-paka. I know this fish is *tapu*. Please...
(pushes the fish toward Noro)
...I am at your mercy.

Haoa tosses his line in the water again. Noro catches his breath.

NORO

No one need hear of this.

He pushes two of the fish back to Haoa and staggers to his feet with the largest one.

Facing page: Grandfather flies the sacred kite as he and Tupa try to interpret its erratic swooping. Above: Moai *at Anakena wearing the red stone "hats."*

« In the past, some scholars have suggested [the *pukao*] represented grass-hats or a kind of turban made of painted paper-mulberry or *tapa* (cylindrical head-dresses are found in much of Polynesia), others that they were dressed and stained top-knots of hair, or wigs: it goes without saying that Von Däniken saw them as space helmets! Red was a significant colour associated with ritual and chiefly power throughout Polynesia, and hair was sometimes coated with red ochreous earth in Melanesia. At present, the most likely explanation is that they are a stylized version of the *hau kurakura*, a red feather head-dress worn by warriors—the early European visitors saw islanders wearing feathers on their heads, and some circular or cylindrical feather head-dresses have actually survived. Throughout Polynesia, red feathers were identified with the spiritual power of the gods. »

Paul Bahn and John Flenley
Easter Island, Earth Island

NORO

For your daughter.

He wobbles off. Haoa smiles ever so slightly.

RANU RARAKU QUARRY

Day

Total blackness. The hammering of stone on stone. Suddenly, light breaks through. The hole gets wider and wider, and then a dusty eye appears. Now a weary Short Ear face fills the hole and shouts triumphantly.

He sticks a rough hand through the hole and an equally rough hand shakes his. They scramble clear and we pull back to reveal the giant *moai* keel and this final perforation in its length.

Laborers shove palm logs along the shelf beside the keel and we crane up to find the Monster strung with heavy ropes—patched-together ropes—and Heke standing on the giant chest. He looks stunned.

HEKE

Replaced?

One of Tupa's priests has brought the news. The Short Ears have fallen behind schedule and Heke must pay the price. Riro is ordered to take charge.

Heke climbs down off his final statue. The other Short Ears witness his humiliation. One of them hands him a basket full of rock debris.

BASKETMAN

Try and forget about it. Go on now—dump this.

Heke takes it, wanders downhill in a daze.

RIRO

Lines ready?

He looks high up the quarry slope where line handlers brace themselves

to take the giant weight on huge, spliced-together ropes wound around tree trunks set in the rock itself.

Far below at the bottom of the slope, a pit—a huge post hole—has been dug to receive the *moai* once it's been lowered.

RIRO

Cut the keel!

Beneath the *moai*, Atta and Make and a dozen other workers slam sharpened tree trunks in and out of the space below the Monster, hammering away at the thin tissue of rock between each perforation.

One breaks. More hammering, and then another goes. Then another, more violently. The statue groans. Everyone pauses... the Monster is coming to life. Tentatively, the workers start hammering again. A few more blows and another perforation shatters.

Then in rapid sequence the remaining ones explode. Stone shrapnel flies everywhere. Wounded hammerers leap from the narrow trench in terror as the vast weight settles onto the palm rollers and rope lines.

In closeup we see the palm rollers compressing unbelievably. Sap runs from them like fresh sugarcane. The ropes stretch and strain, making surreal sounds. Now a few of the huge lines pop and break.

MAKE

Hold...*hold*...

Riro yells to the line handlers.

Facing page: Heke, the master stone carver, is played by Faenza Reuben. Above: The Monster bursts loose from its moorings.

RIRO

Start lowering! Take some pressure off!

What no one sees is Heke, a broken man, wandering onto the waste-strewn slope below the worksite. He spills out his basketload of rock and stares blankly at the great *moai* stretching into the distance along the coast. His glazed eyes turn skyward.

HEKE

...what for?

Up above, another rope snaps. The rollers are practically paste.

RIRO

More rope! More rope!

The crew desperately tries to sling another line around the giant's chin. Make glances downslope, screams.

MAKE

Heke!

Snap! Snap! Snap! The final ropes break and slice through the air like colossal whips. The giant *moai* starts to slide. Everyone dives out of the way except Make, who screams again at Heke. We can't tell if the old man hears Make or the ominous rumbling, but he turns and looks up the slope anyway—as the culmination of his life's work rockets toward him, gouging the earth impossibly. It shears another *moai* in half like styrofoam and thunders on.

Heke doesn't even try to move. The *moai* crushes him as it passes. It bounces, quaking the earth—and amazingly thuds to a halt in the very pit dug for it.

LONG EAR VILLAGE

Day

A procession of grim-faced Short Ears marches down the *moai* road toward the Long Ear village. Make is in the lead. In the village, in front of the Miru *ahu*, a Long Ear chief rants at a priest indignantly.

They look up to see the Short Ears coming. Something about them seems threatening. Word quickly spreads and Long Ears at the village edge cautiously retreat.

As they come under the giant *ahu*'s shadow, some of the Short Ears feel their resolve weaken. Make and a few others remain resolute. They lead the way straight into the central plaza.

Tupa emerges from the Ariki-mau's lodge, paddle in hand. Armed warriors fall in behind him. Defiant, a little nervous, the Short Ears watch the head priest approach as the *matatoa* quietly encircle them. Riro speaks first.

RIRO

We want more.

TUPA

More what?

HITIRENGA

More of everything.

OLD SHORT EAR MAN

There used to be plenty for everyone.

Tupa sizes things up.

TUPA

Yes, well, that was before there were so many of you, wasn't it?

A few other Long Ears and Short Ears trade insults, until a familiar voice interrupts.

GRANDFATHER

It's good to have lots of children....

Everyone turns as he enters the plaza, glancing around at the delegation. His hands are covered with blood.

GRANDFATHER

It honors the ancestors....Why aren't you in the quarry?

Before the Long Ear ahu*, Short Ears celebrate their triumph in winning the right to compete in the Birdman.*

A little cowed by the Ariki-mau, the Short Ears look to Riro.

RIRO

Heke's dead.

GRANDFATHER

Yes, I heard. Terrible thing...terrible.

TUPA

We were just discussing, Ariki, how they want *more* of everything, and it's been pointed out that since there's *more* of everyone—especially them—there is, unfortunately, *less*.

MAKE

Then we want more of what's left.

A timid Short Ear peeks over his fellows and shouts.

TIMID SHORT EAR

Or we're not building any more *moai*!

SECOND SHORT EAR

Including the big one!

There are murmurs of agreement. Grandfather turns to Tupa in shock.

GRANDFATHER

Not finish the *moai*? Are you mad? Have you lost your minds? Everything depends on that!

RIRO

(humbly)

Then we want half the crops, Ariki.

The Long Ear chiefs stir and object.

RIRO

And half the wood for fuel.

THIRD SHORT EAR

And no more hats!

The Long Ears are livid.

Noro tries to convince Grandfather to grant the Short Ears' demands.

RIRO
And one more thing.
(glances at his comrades for courage)
We want to compete for the Bird-man.

A beat.

TUPA
Kill them.

Instantly the Long Ear warriors move in with clubs and spears, ready to strike. Noro, who has been watching the encounter from the edge of the plaza, now speaks up.

NORO
If they're dead, who will build the *moai*?

The *matatoa* pause, look to Tupa for an answer as Noro continues.

NORO
Certainly none of us remember how.

Grandfather curses and flutters his fingernails in frustration. He signals the *matatoa* to back off, turns his back on the crowd.

GRANDFATHER
A word please, Tupa.

Eyeing Noro, Tupa marches over to Grandfather.

GRANDFATHER
I don't need this, priest.
(holds up bloody hands)
I have chicken entrails to read.

TUPA
Let me slay these troublemakers, sire, and make your day serene.

Noro joins them.

NORO
Just give them something, Grand-father. A little food and fuel....

They'll get what they want and so will you—

TUPA
But Short Ears competing for the Birdman, sire? It's—

NORO
You know I'll win, Grandfather. They're all too tired from working to climb and swim. But you've got to let them think they've got a chance at something.

Tupa finally snaps.

TUPA
Forgive me, Ariki-paka, but I don't recall your opinion having been sought.

NORO
Then recall my not caring, priest.

Tupa is stunned, purple with rage.

TUPA
This is unheard of, Ariki. It's bad precedent and—

NORO
Just give them something!

Silence falls.

GRANDFATHER
Why?

NORO
Because I see real danger in all this.

He's very earnest. A multitude of faces awaits Grandfather's word.

GRANDFATHER
Why must everything be so difficult?

He turns to the plaza, addresses the Short Ears.

The Power Behind the Throne

"Tupa's not just a downright, obvious villain," explains actor George Henare, who plays the powerful chief priest of the Miru clan. "He's more subtle and Machiavellian. He wants to rule, of course—but not take the blame for anything that goes wrong, so he positions himself as second in command, where he can control the Ariki-mau. He's the original bureaucrat."

To his screen interpretation of *Rapa Nui*'s "Iago," Henare brings a wealth of stage experience. A member of New Zealand's thriving community of Maori actors, he has performed in more than 200 shows for Auckland's distinguished Mercury Theatre Company —"everything from King Lear to Toad of Toad Hall," as the actor wryly observes. In recognition of a twenty-year career spanning opera, theater, radio plays, and television, Henare recently was awarded an Order of the British Empire by Queen Elizabeth.

Henare relished the role of Tupa, his third feature film portrayal. Learning to wield the heavy ceremonial paddle was no trouble: "We Maoris have a similar weapon, called a *tiayaha*, which I've used on stage." More challenging was the need to "walk a fine line" with his character, and not let Tupa slip over into parody or melodrama. "He keeps his villainy under wraps," Henare says. "He's a man who plays by the rules."

GRANDFATHER

You have broken so many *tapu* today, Make-Make should eat your souls in hell for all eternity....But I'm going to grant these requests on one condition...

The Short Ears light up. The Long Ears are appalled.

GRANDFATHER

For the Short Ears to enter a competitor in the Birdman race, the Great Moai must be finished—*with* a hat—by the time the sunbirds arrive at Motu Nui.

The Short Ears blanch a bit.

GRANDFATHER

...But if he *loses* the race, the Short Ear competitor will be sacrificed to honor the reign of the new Birdman, because of your insolence.... Now, who would swim for the Short Ears?

The Short Ears look at each other. They hadn't counted on this.

MAKE

I will.

Heads turn.

GRANDFATHER

Make...and if you win, who would be your Birdman?

MAKE

Myself.

Grandfather arches an eyebrow at him and flutters his hands.

GRANDFATHER

Fine, back to work now.

MAKE

I make one last condition, Ariki-mau.

GRANDFATHER

(out of patience)
What?!

MAKE

If the Great Moai is finished in time, and if I swim for and win the Birdman...the girl in the Virgin Cave is my bride.

Noro locks eyes with him. Tupa loves it.

TUPA

That seems fair.

Grandfather seeks expedience.

GRANDFATHER

Agreed. Just finish the *moai* in time.

He takes his leave, followed by grinning Tupa and the warriors, stopping Noro's protest with a bloody, upraised hand. The joyous Short Ears start their chant.

SHORT EARS

Make...Make...Make...

His defiant look to Noro is broken by hands slapping him on the back.

From the boat ramp where he has been repairing a canoe, Haoa has witnessed everything. Make now approaches him with the bold crowd in tow, extends his hand like a sincere comrade, and invites Haoa to train "his future son-in-law" for the Birdman. Haoa politely declines and—looking at Noro—says he's already promised someone else.

AROUND THE ISLAND

Night and the following dawn

As the Short Ears celebrate their triumph and hail their new champion, Make announces that he will work with them throughout the coming days to finish the great *moai* on time—and train for the Birdman at night. To demonstrate his commitment, he immediately takes off on a hard run out of the crater and along the coast, through the palm grove, and past the Virgin Cave at Orongo.

As dawn breaks, he races along another clifftop, headed back to the quarry. We pan with him until he disappears behind Haoa's head, in the foreground, watching him. Haoa turns to Noro with a frown.

HAOA

How bad do you want to win?

Noro stands above the windy surf, wet and shivering, retching and breathless.

NORO

More than anything.

Haoa points at Make's disappearing figure.

HAOA

Enough to see him sacrificed?

NORO

I guess.

HAOA

No more guessing. If you win, Make dies. Accept that. Believe me...he has.

Noro nods, sets his jaw. Haoa pulls out a clay "egg."

HAOA

Your future. From now on, you wear it whenever you climb or swim.

He ties the egg to Noro's forehead with a *tapa* headband.

As the weeks pass and the time of the Birdman draws nearer, those with a stake in the outcome intensify their efforts. Noro and Make pursue their grueling training routines, Noro driven by Haoa's prodding and thoughts of Ramana, Make running and swim-

Haoa fastens the clay "egg" in its special carrying pouch to Noro's forehead.

Noro clings to the slippery cliff after a training swim.

ming and climbing for his very life—and his people's future.

The Short Ears gradually tilt the Monster *moai* upright, raising it with log levers inch by painful inch, then propping it with stones that form a huge ramp. As more stones are added, the statue angles skyward, and a sturdy log sledge is lashed to its base. More logs are laid in parallel down the slope beneath the quarry, joining the debris-strewn road to the coast. The sound of chopping fills the air all day long in the palm groves, as more trees are cut…and still more.

THE MONSTER'S PIT

Dawn

Backlit by a pink horizon, Make approaches from the coast. We pull back to find the Monster fully erect on its sled, like some prehistoric space shuttle waiting to be moved to the launch pad. Workers swarm over its back, chipping away at the remains of the keel and fastening spliced-together *totora* ropes.

A dozen scrap wood fires illuminate the scene as Make arrives—wet, hands and feet cut from climbing, his face as hard as the *moai*. Tired as they are, the other Short Ears cheer him. Riro hands him a piece of sugarcane.

RIRO

Ready.

Make moves to the back of the *moai* where the roller crew waits.

MAKE
Let's go.

Together they begin to lever the sled. The guy lines tighten.

MAKE
One, two, three. Push!

The roller crew heaves until their faces turn blue, but nothing happens. Others move to the sled and add what muscle they can.

Closeup on the log rollers, which finally, imperceptibly, begin to budge. The crew strains harder until the wood actually squeals. The rollers churn, shredding themselves and the log road. Against the rising sun, the Monster is moving at last.

THE *MOAI* ROAD

Morning

Short Ear women and children—the road gang—clear loose stones out of the path for the approaching Monster. They're actually widening the old road to accommodate its massive girth. Men follow the road crew, laying parallel palm logs that are frayed from use.

We shift to a closeup of the *moai* sled making progress at a snail's pace, grinding the rollers underneath. As it

With the Monster finally upright, Short Ears begin to drag it inch by painful inch toward its destination in the Long Ear village.

gouges past, the parallel logs are pried from the ground. Those that survive are moved ahead for further abuse. The wrecked ones are discarded for firewood to light the way at night. New logs arrive constantly.

Make watches the crew on the sled. Hard and haggard, he chews a *kumara* as Riro and some workers approach.

RIRO
(holds out scrap wood)
We're running out of logs. The weight breaks them and the friction grinds them to dust.

MAKE
Then grease them.

RIRO
With what? We've nothing left.

Make looks down at the *kumara* in his hand, and shoves it between the sled and rollers. Instantly mashed, it slickens the wood, lessens the wear. Make takes another from a worker's mouth even as the man levers.

MAKE
With these. Cut the ration.

All eyes stare at him. Make indicates the Monster.

MAKE
Nothing else matters.

He moves off. Atta starts collecting everybody's breakfast.

MONTAGE
Day and Night

Short Ears strain at their ropes and levers. Some furtively lick crushed *kumara* off the rollers as they pass.... Noro lies on the ground, protecting the egg lashed to his head as Haoa circles around him, kicking viciously. ...Make, his fingers gripping a rocky overhang, struggles to do another pullup....More scrap wood is thrown on a roadside fire. Wreathed in sparks, the giant *moai* glides by against a full moon. Carvers chip away at the back of its head as it passes....In the palm grove, another tree falls, is hauled away....

The Monster's inexorable progress is never slowed. Soon the Short Ears are a hundred meters from the Long Ear *ahu*.

GRANDFATHER'S LODGE
Day

Through the front door, Tupa watches the Monster being elevated onto the *ahu* by a growing ramp. He's amazed and worried by the Short Ears' progress, and raises with Grandfather the unthinkable possibility that a Short Ear could actually win the Birdman.

Grandfather, his eyes wild and sunken, scoffs at this, claims that Noro's victory is certain.

TUPA
We must speak of your grandson, Ariki-mau. I think you place too much confidence in him.

GRANDFATHER
Noro?

TUPA
Win or lose, he is the next Miru chief, but—forgive me, sire—your grandson is not cut from the same stone as yourself. He's unruly. He lives to disappoint....I fear he is more like his father, the blasphemer, than yourself.

Grandfather remembers, draws a melancholy breath.

GRANDFATHER
My son...blasphemer....I had such plans for that boy. How could he not believe, Tupa? How?

TUPA
Bad seed, that's all. And bad seed needs a strong hand. Someone trusted, like myself, to guide his careless ways in strange times like these—or even to replace him should he suffer, say, some untimely tragic death.

Grandfather's wavering focus goes back out the window to the brooding *moai*. He sees a burial party placing freshly washed bones in a chamber beneath the *ahu*.

GRANDFATHER
Tell me I won't be just another skull under the *ahu*, Tupa. Tell me you won't be making fish hooks from my thighbones. The White Canoe—that's my destiny...isn't it?

Tupa assures him that wondrous things are surely to come.

PALM GROVE

Day

A sea of tree stumps on a barren slope, and in its midst—a single standing palm. A figure sleepwalks through this scene of destruction: Noro on his training run. He can't believe his eyes.

The palm's trunk is scarred from the work that's gone on here. But you can still see old childlike glyphs carved in the bark by Noro and Make, and the more recent ones by Noro and Ramana.

Noro slumps against the tree as a group of Short Ears approaches from down the slope. Riro, a few others ...and Make out in front. Noro notes the stone adzes in their hands.

MAKE
Don't worry, Golden Boy—we've only come for the tree.

Make hardens himself for the climbing part of the race with countless rock pullups.

As they move forward, Noro jumps in front of the palm.

NORO
Are you crazy? It's the last one! There's no more after this! You can't cut down the last tree!

RIRO
Somebody's going to. Why shouldn't it be us?

Make and other Short Ears, adzes at the ready, grimly approach the grove where the last palm tree stands.

Noro grabs at their adzes as they start to swing, fights them, wraps himself around the palm trunk.

NORO
Just leave it! Just one!

Finally Riro and the others peel him off, wrestle him to the ground as Make begins to chop.

NORO
No!

He watches his and Ramana's marks disintegrate under the blows as the adze viciously tears it apart.

The last tree in the world crashes to the ground. Without a second thought, the Short Ears start dragging the log down the slope, leaving Noro trembling with rage and irrevocable loss.

HAOA'S CAVE

Night

Noro stares bitterly into the flames of Haoa's scrap fire.

HAOA
Once we were great navigators. We fished deep waters in great canoes. ...That's lost forever now.
(a deep breath)
The Birdman can't make trees grow back, but he can try to fix what's left.

NORO
Haoa, why did my father leave? Was he crazy, like everyone says?

HAOA
You've seen where the craziness is.

NORO
But where was he sailing? There's no place to go. All the other lands have sunk.

HAOA
He had to see for himself.

NORO
Even if it killed him?

HAOA
Your father was restless, and when your mother died having you, everything here stopped making sense to him.

Haoa moves to a niche in the cave, returns with a large, strange shape.

HAOA
Then one day, in a tidepool, he found this.

Closeup on an ancient piece of wood sparring, covered with dead barnacles—flotsam from some unknown source. As Noro turns it in his hands with wonderment, a rusty ring comes off in his fingers.

NORO
Is it made by the gods?

Surrounded by a sea of stumps, the lone tree awaits its fate.

HAOA
Or some sort of men.

NORO
Then it has to be from the sunken lands, doesn't it?...Doesn't it?

Electrified, Noro looks seaward.

NORO
Did he tell Grandfather?

HAOA
He tried to.

NORO
I've always been ashamed of him, Haoa.

HAOA
Know this—your father loved you, and his *mana* will guide you someday, some way.

ORONGO AND POIKE

Night

At the Virgin Cave, Noro and Ramana share another tender, painful visit. She tells him of a dream she's had: of the two of them walking in the sun and lying together by their special tree in the palm grove. He can't bear to tell her of its fate.

Make, training near the opposite side of the island, is climbing a cliff when he spots the rock-and-feather marker of forbidden territory—the slopes of Poike. Climbing toward the marker, he discovers a lava tube cave that leads through the cliff, growing wider and finally emerging at the base of a hill, right in the heart of the *tapu* landscape.

Haoa shows Noro the broken spar found by his father: evidence of other people "out there" somewhere.

He makes another discovery. Someone has built a fortification here: a huge ditch camouflaged by brush and filled with scrap wood and sharpened stakes. Nearby is a cache of weapons and food. Make grabs a bite as he leaves...with plenty of food for thought.

AROUND THE ISLAND

Day

From the windswept islet of Motu Nui, we look back at the main island. A shape swoops through the air. Then another...and another. The sound of waves now gives way to the sound of *manutara* birds.

The birds swoop and hover over Motu Nui. Atop the Orongo cliff, near the site of the birdman petroglyphs, a priest observes their arrival. He turns, walks to a ledge above the massive Rano Kao crater, presses his mouth to the hole in a stone horn, and blows. The sound reverberates from the crater.

Across the barren hills and plains of stumps in the palm grove, Noro sits on what's left of the Tree, gazing in wonder at a *manutara* bird hovering overhead.

NORO

Where do you come from?...and where do you go?...

He heads for the sound of the horn.

At the Long Ear village Make, hearing the call as well, stands up from behind the crown of a scoria topknot. Far below him, the Long Ears emerge from their huts and stream toward the beckoning sound. Make brushes one last bit of stone dust from the topknot, grabs a *tapa* rope, and starts shimmying down.

Just as Make lands, Grandfather's litter appears with Tupa and the whole entourage.

GRANDFATHER

Finished?

Make nods. Long Ears and Short Ears hold their breath. Grandfather steps back, his eyes moving up the Monster, backlit by the morning sun. He's standing in a shadow two hundred yards long. The *moai* dwarfs everything else on the Long Ear *ahu*.

Grandfather's eyes scan the ocean horizon. It's empty. Tears well up in his sunken eyes as he slowly shakes his head.

GRANDFATHER

(sighing, shrugging)

It's not enough...I guess.

You can almost hear blood curdling in the Short Ears' veins.

GRANDFATHER

(to Make)

But you may compete.

With a rousing cheer, the Short Ears hoist Make off his feet and head for Orongo, leaving Grandfather looking small and lost in their wake.

RANO KAU CRATER

Twilight, the evening before the race

The three islets of Motu Nui, Motu Iti, and Motu Kao Kao can be seen through the gap in the crater rim. At the ceremonial village high atop Orongo, the pre-race ritual is about to begin. Hundreds of torches approach from along the ridge.

Led by dancers costumed as bird figures, the Long Ears stream past the three old *moai* to the central plaza, laughing and shouting. Everyone is dressed and painted for a celebration. Each clan is led by its champion.

A torch is tossed on the huge central bonfire, and the revelry begins. Half-naked dancers whirl around the blazing fire, making inviting gestures to the crowd.

Each clan feasts from baskets they have brought, making a big show of what little food they have. The Short Ears just watch, stomachs growling.

Each competitor sits before his potential Birdman—a Long Ear chief—while priests recite charms from *rongorongo* tablets in his behalf. Others apply paint to the racers in the the colors of their clan.

Here and there, sweating couples slip into the dark. A man and a woman lasciviously pass an "egg" be-

Make shimmies down the moai *after putting the finishing touches on top.*

A night of frenzied ceremony precedes the start of the Bird-man ritual.

tween their mouths. This is fertility worship at its finest. Grandfather watches the whole spectacle blearily.

GRANDFATHER
Good, good...more babies...more everything! That's what we need...
(looks heavenward)
...isn't it?

Noro, painted a dull yellow, sits at Grandfather's feet.

He stares through the flames at Make, who sits motionless as the Short Ear women color their champion with the only paint they can find—charcoal. Black as night, Make glares back at Noro.

ORONGO
The next morning

The clans assemble on the crater's knife edge behind their painted champions. Tupa stands before them, declaiming the traditional instructions to the waiting competitors.

TUPA
...to descend these heights,
(pointing)
to swim to Motu Nui, and to find the first *manutara* egg. Then to swim that egg back, to carry it up the cliffs, and present it unbroken into your Bird-man candidate's hand...

The competitors grease up, make final adjustments to their *totora* floats, their headbands. Makita and Ngaara smile coldly at each other. Over to one side, a group of Long Ears are placing bets.

An odd creaking sound becomes audible over Tupa's droning. It is coming from above the Virgin Cave, where priests are hoisting Ramana's cage up from the cliff. Tupa has saved this bit of drama for the last possible minute. Make and Noro are locked breathlessly onto the sound.

TUPA

(smiling nastily)

...and for two of you there is also this...

The cage at last creaks into view. A huddled figure sits within, her back to us. A tattered, filthy cloak is pulled up to cover her head. Now the priests swing the cage around and open the door—revealing a phantom. Ramana's skin is eerily translucent, her lips cracked, her eyes beneath her matted hair squinched tight against the sunlight.

The priests help her from the cage. She can barely stand and when she smiles in triumph, her trembling teeth look terrible. Her voice is a cracked whisper.

RAMANA

I did it.

The crowd's silence momentarily breaks Grandfather's trancelike gaze toward the horizon. He glances over at Ramana.

GRANDFATHER

Huh?...Oh, yes, very nice. Wash her up...stretch those ears...

(fluttering his hands)

...let's get on with it.

Make is beside himself, as is Noro. Reeling from Ramana's condition and Grandfather's cavalier indifference to it, he turns and gets right in the old man's blank face.

Just before the start of the race, Ramana is released from her long ordeal in the Virgin Cave.

NORO

Matua Tane...if I win, you retire. It's time for a new Ariki-mau.

Noro backs away and takes his place among the waiting competitors, leaving Grandfather stunned. After a long moment, Tupa leans in with a stage whisper.

TUPA

Say *"Go."*

Grandfather blinks, flutters his hands.

GRANDFATHER

Go.

A wild cheer erupts as the competitors, floats on their backs, bolt onto the narrow crater ridge. They navigate the knife edge dangerously fast in single file, looking for a place to start down.

The big, imposing Makita is out in front, until Ngaara suddenly shoves him. Makita instantly falls about nine hundred feet to his death.

One of the boldly painted Birdman competitors picks his way carefully down the cliff.

THIRD LONG EAR CHIEF
(*incredulous, to First Long Ear Chief*)
He pushed him! Your Ngaara pushed my man!

FIRST LONG EAR CHIEF
(*proud*)
He's a winner.

Tupa trades a wink with him. More bets change hands.

Ngaara is the first to start hand over hand down the precipice. The other racers collect themselves and start after him. We pull back to a long shot of the immense black cliff, small specks of color scrambling over it. Then zoom in close to tough, calloused feet leaping from foothold to foothold. Hands fly over the rock. The speed is unbelievably breakneck. Make and Noro race through the foreground, passing Pure White. They're gaining on Ngaara.

The slope eases and a switchback trail appears. Ngaara jumps onto it, but both Make and Noro continue straight down, passing him. From a viewpoint right up against the rock face, we look down to the smashing ocean three hundred feet below. The last hundred feet look completely sheer.

As Make and Noro exchange a seething look, Make tumbles on a loose slope, head over heels, and starts sliding on his back. He manages to get the *totora* float under him and rides it like a banana sled until he can finally get his feet planted near the bottom. Scraped up but uninjured, he stands—and sees that his float is completely shredded.

Noro decides on another route. He swings over and gets a handhold, but when he starts to swing again, the rock he's gripping gives way. His fingernails claw the perpendicular face as he slides, trying to keep from free-falling. One little ledge lies between him and a sheer, hundred-foot drop to the rocky beach.

His toes catch and he falls over backwards, landing with his head hanging over the ledge. Far below, from different routes, the other competitors are entering the water.

On the beach, holding his shredded float, Make looks around wildly. Then he notices Makita's body bobbing at the water's edge…next to his intact float. Make races for it.

Noro gauges his situation. There's absolutely no way down the hundred foot drop, and backtracking to find another route will cost him precious minutes. He doesn't hesitate. Unslinging his float, he hurls it as far out as he can. As it hits the surging water among the swimmers, Noro launches himself like a bird into the wind.

He explodes beneath the surface and arcs upward. Surfacing just past the giant swells, he climbs aboard his float—right in the middle of the swimmers.

The wonderstruck spectators cheer madly, and the bets change again.

The camera tracks Half & Half and Mudcolor churning through the water. Stroking powerfully, Noro pulls even with them. We cut to Ngaara—a good swimmer but not great. Make starts to pass him, staying well out of his angry reach. Pure White windmills past them both.

Now a dark form swims ominously right over the lens—a shark.

On the Orongo clifftop, Grandfather squints into the distance.

GRANDFATHER

The Short Ear—Make—he's swimming strong.

(turns to Tupa)

What was it we promised him?

TUPA

The girl in the cave.

Stunned, Ramana listens blindly.

Back in the ocean, the swimmers cleave past the camera, all of them desperate for breath. A sea-level view of Moto Nui ahead shows where the weird, ancient lava-flow slopes meet crashing water.

Float camera closeup on Noro's face as he blasts through a wave, zeroing in on a landing. Timing is everything. Already Pure White is out of the water. Using his float for a bumper, Noro rides a wave into the rocks, and hangs on.

MOTU NUI

Approaching midday

The exhausted swimmers sling their floats across their backs and slog up the vast rippled rock. At the top of the islet they barely pause before

Above: The "float camera" captures Noro cleaving through the waves. Facing page, top: Long Ears, in foreground, cheer on their favorites while the Short Ears watch in silence. Bottom: Mudcolor, holding an egg, shouts back to his chief on the clifftop.

plunging into the deep grass filled with squawking birds.

A bird sitting on its nest is pushed away by Make—but he finds no egg. He whirls, searching onward. Another competitor runs down a nesting bird, shooing it off. There lies an egg! Mudcolor jumps up triumphantly, holds the prize aloft, and shouts toward Orongo.

MUDCOLOR
Shave your head, Ataranga! I have the egg!

Mudcolor turns for the water and runs straight into Ngaara. Who breaks his arm with a vicious blow, and takes his egg.

Now Pure White finds an egg. Then, in quick succession, Make, Half & Half, and Noro. All hastily fasten the precious cargo to their forehead pouch rigs, looking over their shoulders for pursuers.

Ngaara blocks the lava slope as he struggles with his headband. Pure White gives him a wide berth but slips against a sharp rock, wincing in pain. We see his thigh laid open as he jumps back in the water.

Make gets past Ngaara with a well-placed kick. Noro doesn't even try. Without pausing he veers right and leaps off the lava shelf. In midair, he unslings the float and cups his forehead before hitting the water.

Shift to a close shot as Ngaara claws the water, and track ahead to find Noro, then Make, and in the lead Pure White. Blood streams from his cut leg. He's too tired to see the fin and glistening back of the shark rising and sinking beside him.

On the surface, Pure White is

suddenly jolted. He turns and sees that his leg is a spewing stump. As he starts to scream, his whole body is yanked beneath the roiling surface.

Second Long Ear Chief goes white.

FIRST LONG EAR CHIEF
...And he was doing so well!

Noro and Make pull up in fear, eyeing the bloody froth around Pure White's bitten float, and each other. Ngaara never hesitates. Make sets his face and surges forward. Noro follows.

In a high angle shot looking down the Orongo cliff, the yellow, black, and red figures surf toward the stony beach. They sweep into shore and hit the ground running, abandoning the floats. Without a moment's pause they assault the cliff.

CROWD
Three left! Black, yellow, red!

TUPA
(nervous)
This should be interesting.

Three figures steam up the black cliff face, exactly even. Noro scrambles right toward the camera; then Make and Ngaara do the same. Every upward effort one of them makes is immediately matched by the other two. Teeth gritted, hearts exploding, they're almost delirious with pain. A pure test of wills.

On the clifftop, Ramana tries to glean information from the cacophony of shouting bettors and fans. She can't see the Short Ears watching in anxious silence, or Grandfather glancing at them. But she can hear.

GRANDFATHER
And what happens if the Short Ear loses?

TUPA
(no patience)
He dies.

The climbers are about two hundred feet from the top. Right between Noro and Make, Ngaara flags ever so slightly, falls behind. As his chief screams at him to do something, Ngaara desperately lunges after the other two and grabs their legs. He starts trying to yank them off the cliff. Noro and Make kick and flail, trying to hang onto the rock while protecting their precious eggs. They cannot break Ngaara's iron grip.

As Ngaara is pulling himself farther up Make's leg, Noro reaches down and grabs his topknot, lifting him by his hair while gripping the cliff with his other hand. With a pained roar, Ngaara lets go of Make and claws for Noro, who desperately screams at his former friend.

NORO

Hit him! *Help me!*

A beat. Make takes off up the cliff.

The Long Ears are stunned and the hungry Short Ears levitated by cheers.

Ngaara rips at the yellow arm holding him by the hair. With adrenaline and sheer animal strength, Noro slams the raging red man into the cliff until he goes limp enough for Noro to turn him loose. Then he looks up, already climbing.

Make is fifty feet above him, nearly to the top. He can hear the cheers.

SHORT EARS

Make!...Make!...Make!

Make reaches the final ledge and pauses, overcome by emotion as much as exhaustion. He sees that Noro cannot catch him and loves the pain in his striving face. He takes the perfect egg from his headband, looks down the cliff and out to Motu Nui, savoring the moment he's worked so hard for, locking it in his memory forever.

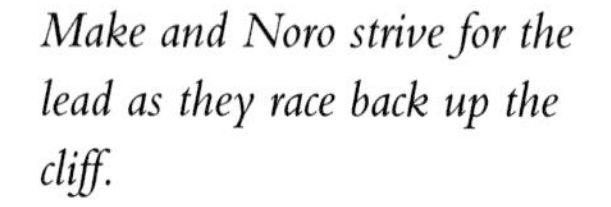

Make and Noro strive for the lead as they race back up the cliff.

Make lurches up over the ledge. Trips, and drops his egg.

Time stops as he sees the broken yolk seeping into the ground. He looks up in despair at the Short Ears. Riro shrieks with rage and frustration. Tupa smiles.

Behind Make, Noro crawls over the edge of the cliff, stands and realizes what's happened. He carefully unfurls his headband, removes his intact egg and advances through the wails and cheers.

So daunting and resolute is Noro's approach that Grandfather actually cowers a bit. His exhausted, scarred grandson marches right up to him, stoops...and tenderly wraps the egg in Ramana's hand.

RAMANA

...Noro?

NORO

I did it. I won.

Like any good weathervane, Tupa knows which way the wind is blowing and leads the applause. Noro reaches to take Ramana in his arms. That's when he realizes she's at least eight months pregnant. Make just watches them, his anguish bottomless.

The egg splats beside them as Grandfather bumps into Ramana. The old man is making strangled noises, and his eyes are wide. He's obviously having some sort of seizure, and now his shaking arm extends.

GRANDFATHER

...Wh...c...white canoe...!

Tupa smiles patronizingly, then does a double-take. En masse, the crowd turns and gazes far out on the slate grey sea, where a gigantic albino shape rises out of the water. Barely moving, bigger than Motu Nui, it exudes majesty and ethereal power.

Triumph and hope drain out of Make like the broken egg through his fingers.

It's an iceberg. Beckoning. Like Halley's comet...the Shroud of Turin...some alien spaceship.

GRANDFATHER

The White Canoe!!

The crowd tries to comprehend what they're looking at. Open-mouthed, they turn to each other for answers. Led by Grandfather, they surge from Orongo in amazement, scrambling for any kind of float or boat they can find.

ON THE OCEAN

Day

From sea level the iceberg is even more imposing and inexplicable, as an armada of reed canoes cautiously heads toward it. In the royal canoe—an ancient, cobwebbed wooden relic—Grandfather sits at the prow. He wears his grandest garb, and his eyes are full of faith and madness.

Behind him ride Noro and Ramana, Tupa, and a few overwhelmed priests. The ceremonial vessel is followed by an aquatic array of nervous Long Ear nobility and baffled Short Ears. Hundreds more people line the shore in the background.

Bare feet clamber up the side of the berg. Grandfather is helped over the top edge and stands with his shivering, frightened entourage of priests and chiefs and wives. They shift from foot to cold foot. Rapturous, Grandfather moves among them, taking in the endless white.

GRANDFATHER
Where are the paddles?

No one knows. He shrugs, ecstatic nevertheless. A priest baby-steps over to Grandfather, forcing a smile.

FIRST PRIEST
Ariki-mau, are we sure this is...

GRANDFATHER
Yes, we are. Where's Noro? Tupa?

He walks to the edge and looks down. Noro and Tupa bob in the royal canoe.

GRANDFATHER
Aren't you coming?

NORO
Ramana's sick, Grandfather. I...I can't leave her.

GRANDFATHER
Priest?

Tupa beautifully feigns enormous pain and sacrifice.

TUPA
All my life I've waited for just this day, Ariki...but someone must guide the new Ariki-mau...

Noro looks at him.

TUPA
...until you send for us.

Deified, Grandfather reaches out to the boats.

GRANDFATHER
Anyone else? Long Ear, Short Ear?

A resounding crack and roar answer him, and all heads turn to see a huge chunk of ice calving off the farthest end of the berg. The canoes bounce in the giant wash. The awed, terrified people make no move toward this transport to heaven. Grandfather sadly shakes his head at them.

GRANDFATHER
What did you think salvation would look like?

A final few Short Ears dash for the berg with hands and broken paddles. They clamber aboard as Grandfather waves goodbye, tears streaming down his face. Finally he's going to see God.

A great chanting and wailing rises from the berg and the boats as fate and patched-up paddles pull them apart.

BIRDMAN HOUSE

Twilight

Faint streaks of yellow paint still line Noro's exhausted, staring, competely insensate face. High on a slope above the Long Ear village, he and Ramama sit before the Birdman house. He holds the Birdman's feathered stick.

Far out on the twilight horizon, the icy monolith disappears in silhouette. They stare at the once-in-a-millennium phenomenon.

RAMANA
Is it gone...Noro?

NORO
Yes, it's gone.

RAMANA
Good. Maybe we can live our lives as we choose now.

She pushes back her hood and tilts her face up, hopeful.

RAMANA
Do you think I'm more beautiful?

Noro can't disguise the pain as he looks at her.

NORO
You've always been beautiful to me.

RAMANA
Then why haven't you kissed me yet?

He presses his lips to hers, trying to mean it, but Ramana can feel his numbness.

RAMANA
(softly)
You didn't tell me Make was swimming too...and that he's to die.

NORO
You didn't tell me about the child.

RAMANA
Is there anything else I should know? ...Another girl? It seems like everything has changed...somehow.

COAST AND RANU RARAKU
Evening

Far below, behind the Long Ear village and *ahu*, hundreds of people stand and kneel at the waterline, silently watching the iceberg vanish.

In the quarry, the wide-eyed Short Ears huddle around a fire, breathlessly speculating.

FISHERWOMAN
Does...does this mean Make-Make is about to descend on us—to eat our souls for doubting?

They pull closer to the fire, scared of the shadows.

THIRD SHORT EAR
Earlier, I'm sure I saw the *moai* on the Hamea *ahu* breathing!

The Short Ears spin, warily watching the stone giants around them. The flickering fire seems to animate them.

An old Short Ear screams and points. Tupa strolls out of the darkness accompanied by two jumpy *matatoa* warriors and his deadly paddle. He smiles, points at Make in the shadows.

TUPA
He lost. I've come for his head...and

Grandfather's ancient royal canoe draws near the iceberg, attended by smaller canoes and people on floats.

to tell you about the new *moai* we're starting tomorrow.

THIRD SHORT EAR
New *moai*? We're through with all that.

Tupa whirls and kills him with a single paddle stroke.

TUPA
Oh, we're just getting started. You saw what happened today—the gods kept their promise. The Long Ear *mana* proved its power...So we're going to build bigger and bigger *moai* until the gods favor us again—with one little difference.

He turns in profile, strokes his goatee.

TUPA
From now on, all *moai* will have beards.

There is a soft *thunk*. Tupa looks down in surprise at a long obsidian spearpoint sticking out of his stomach. He keels over, revealing black-streaked Make. Before the two *matatoa* can take their startled eyes off the dead priest, Make has clubbed them both to death with Tupa's paddle.

Blazing defiance, Make stands before his clan. The Short Ears are shell-shocked, mortified.

FIRST SHORT EAR
But...he is Miru! They are Long Ear!

MAKE
Are you with me?

A beat. Atta steps forward, pulls the spear from Tupa's back, and slices off Tupa's long earlobes. He holds them up, smiling.

Facing page: At the Birdman house, Noro and Ramana try to make sense of the recent strange and terrible events. Above: Make dispatches Tupa with a spear seized from a Long Ear warrior.

ATTA

Not anymore.

Suddenly the Short Ears realize that anything is possible.

BIRDMAN HOUSE

Night

Noro and Ramana lie huddled outside the hut, sleeping, their faces troubled with dreams. Distant screams jar Noro awake. Down on the coast, he sees torches racing into the moonlit Long Ear village. Houses go up in flames. More screams and shouts reach across the night.

Ramana awakens as Noro leaps to his feet. Now she hears the distant chaos too. He tells her that he must go to the aid of the village—he is the Ariki-mau, after all—and she begs to come. He reminds her that she cannot see and would be in great danger, promises that he'll return for her as soon as he can.

LONG EAR VILLAGE

Night

Noro arrives in the aftermath of the main Short Ear assault. Flames and bodies are everywhere. A priest lies clutching the spear that killed him. Noro slips through the village from house to burning house as screaming, blackened Short Ears loot and flee in the background.

Noro sees Long Ears crouched in shadows atop the *ahu*. Glancing around warily, he races across the plaza and up the ramp to where the village survivors huddle beneath their *moai*, protected by the *matatoa* warriors who haven't been killed.

They frantically describe the ferocity of the attack. The Short Ears left to look for Noro, they report, but will soon be back for the rest of them.

One of the priests draws close, his arms and ears slashed. He tries to whisper so no one else can hear.

SECOND PRIEST

(breathless)

There's a place. Safe place. Just for us, Ariki-mau.

NORO

Where?

SECOND PRIEST

The Poike.

NORO

Poike? *Tapu* won't stop them now.

SECOND PRIEST

It's not just *tapu*. It's a fort. Tupa built it.

He tells Noro that Tupa has been killed. Noro thinks for a moment, then instructs the priest to take the remaining Long Ears to Poike. He races back to the Birdman house to get Ramana—but finds her gone. Make has beaten him there.

POIKE PENINSULA

Dawn

The sky is grey and ominous over the vast plateau of Putatikei Volcano. On one side, it drops hundreds of sheer feet into the sea. A long line of antlike Long Ears hurries along the cliff edge, avoiding the dangerously open slope.

The Second Priest knocks over the *tapu* marker, and reassures them that they may pass. He glances warily back toward the rest of the island as Noro runs to intercept them—alone. The priest's look says: "I told you so." They join the others hustling down the slope toward the camouflaged ditch.

The bleached firewood and deadly pointed stakes of the ditch are revealed as the *matatoa* pull the camouflaging brush away. Noro is amazed.

SECOND PRIEST
You see—only one way in or out. The cliffs on three sides. Even with this...unexpected crowd...we've got enough food to hide out for weeks, if the Short Ears don't find us—which they shouldn't.

NORO
And then what—when the food runs out?

SECOND PRIEST
By then, hopefully, the Short Ears will have starved...and we can start over again.

A *matatoa* lookout is pointing. Up on the ridge, tiny lights appear. Torches: a dozen...two dozen...now hundreds. Headed through the *tapu* boundary markers. The Short Ears, guided by Make, have found them.

THIRD LONG EAR CHIEF
The gods have forsaken us for doubting.

NORO
We have forsaken ourselves! No gods did it—we did.

His anger is stunning as he turns to the priests.

NORO
I hate everything you stand for.
(points at distant torches)
...but what they intend is no better.

He wields his war club bitterly.

NORO
So fight—to kill what we've become—and hope someone with sense lives.

Fire is passed from torch to torch as armed Long Ears wait to set the ditch alight. Behind them, women and children pass out weapons from the stores and watch nervously as the sea of Short Ears rolls down the slope.

The Long Ear village burns in the wake of the Short Ears' attack.

Short Ears with torches race to surround the Long Ears at the Poike Ditch.

Now their thudding feet and wild whooping can be heard. A hundred yards away, the flaming Short Ear wave splits—half surging behind a low ridge to the right, half disappearing behind rocks to the left.

Then silence. A lone figure stumbles from behind the low ridge and moves blindly to the open ground in front of the ditch. Ramana squints in the dark, calls to Noro. Finally he answers—knowing he is giving the exact position away. But her questions are heartbreaking.

RAMANA
Was I not white enough? Unacceptable? Is that why you didn't come back?

NORO
I did come back.

RAMANA
(doesn't believe him)
Six moons, Noro—in the dark—trying to be something I'm not!...How long was I supposed to wait this time?

From the sea cave Make discovered, Short Ear silhouettes creep out and start climbing the cliffs. They grab spears and clubs from the Long Ear weapons cache as they sneak past.

RAMANA
Am I Short Ear or Long Ear? I don't know where I fit anymore!...Make loves me, Noro...Said he'll love me no matter what...

NORO
Will he love our child? Ask him that! Ask him what he'll do when it's born!

From the darkness behind the Long Ears comes a voice:

MAKE
I will kill it.

Now a roar is heard and out of the

night descends a wall of charcoal black demons. All you can see are their snarling teeth and vengeful eyes—and the torches they light their spears with. Noro and the Long Ears whirl to meet the onslaught. Behind them on the other side of the ditch, Short Ears rush from behind the hills and torch the wood.

Her purpose served, a horrified Ramana is dragged out of the way by Short Ear women who leap and laugh, brandishing crude weapons. Noro hurries the Long Ear women and children behind him and the *matatoa*, squeezing them against the now blazing ditch.

Flaming spears find their targets. Long Ears drop left and right. The *matatoa* fight back fiercely with clubs and *mataa* blades...but there are far too many Short Ears. They force the Long Ear line back and back—toward the ditch, now a giant earth oven.

Some Long Ears fall into the flaming ditch and stagger out the other side, hair and clothing ablaze. Some fall, some run and twist in agony. The Short Ear women rush from the dark, club them to death. More Long Ears are speared and clubbed, shoved into the fire—including women and kids.

Noro and the *matatoa* fight desperately, trying to protect the women and children. But one by one they are overwhelmed. Noro races through the carnage, seeking Ramana. As he yells to her across the ditch, a club knocks him senseless from behind.

A Short Ear runs up to finish Noro off with a knife. Make steps into the frame and stays his hand.

MAKE

Not yet.

The Short Ear grins, drags Noro away. Laughing Short Ears collect the Long Ear dead from both sides of the ditch and throw them into the smelter.

We crane down to the near end of the ditch to find Noro on his knees with his head pulled back by Short Ears, forced to watch his people's mass cremation. Riro walks up to him, shoves a short stone club, a *paoa*, in Noro's face, showing him the weapon he will be killed with.

As Make arrives, Riro steps aside and hands Make the *paoa*. Make looks down at his vanquished foe and ancient friend. Noro faces his executioner with defiant bitterness.

NORO

You've become what you sought to end.

A beat. It's not so much that Make can't bring himself to do it, it's more the power that the gesture gives him. He hands the club back to Riro.

Storyboard art by Rick Newsome depicting how part of the battle was to be staged.

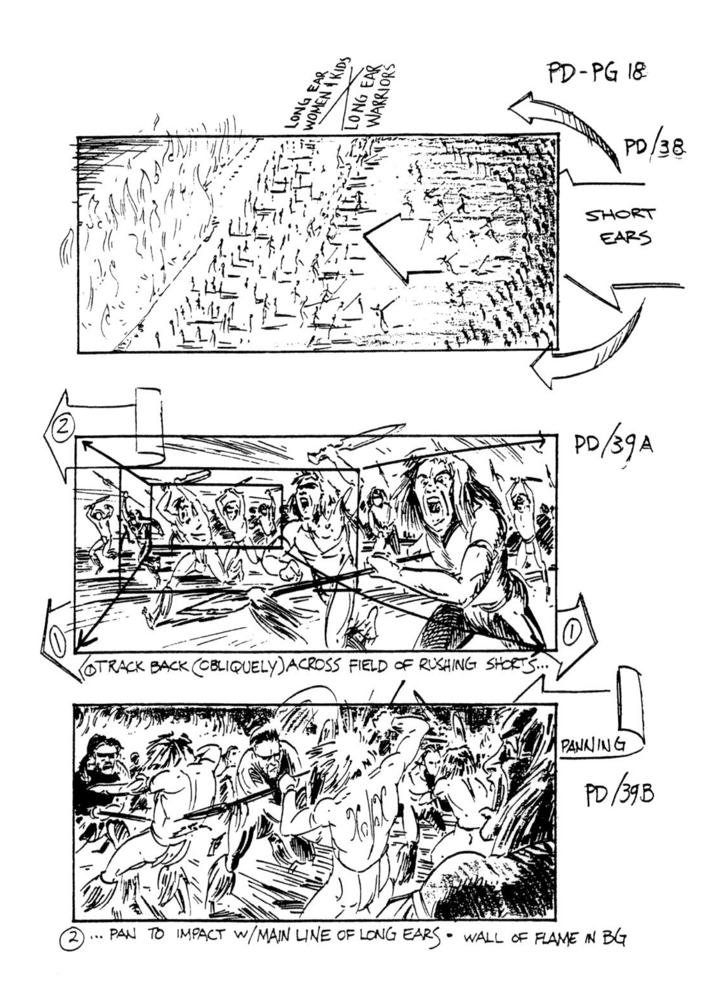

After their bloody victory, vengeful Short Ears pull down the moai *from the Long Ear* ahu.

MAKE
We were friends once, so I'll let you live...
(fierce)
...but we rule now.

LONG EAR VILLAGE

Morning

A *moai* wobbles as frayed ropes pull at it. It slowly topples forward and slams face first into the ground before the Long Ear *ahu*. Carefully positioned rocks make the giant head snap off.

In the background, most of the other *moai* already lie toppled. Amid whoops and cheers, two Short Ears quickly position more stones while their drunken comrades push and pull at another statue behind them.

Noro stumbles past in disbelief, ducking thrown rocks and jeers. He watches another *moai* fall from the *ahu*...then another. The Monster is left for last.

POIKE DITCH

Day

A swirl of smoke and drifting ash. Mad laughter comes from the blackened ditch where Atta and six other Short Ears crouch, working on something. Their eyes are red from smoke, wild from killing. The burned meat they're ripping at isn't chicken.

Make, horrified, protests in vain that this isn't what they fought for. They leave him standing amidst anarchy and ash, the ruler of a world without hope.

PALM GROVE

Day

A cloud of smoke rises in the east. Noro stumbles across an eroded, stump-filled landscape, glancing over his shoulder at distant smoke, with no idea where to go or what to do. Every direction leads to water.

He trips and falls to his hands and knees, trembling, completely spent. Then, unable to contain it any longer, he begins to weep. Deep sobs wrack him over and over...until something catches his lowered eyes. It's the rusty ring from the ship wreckage, swinging on a cord around his neck.

Noro grips the necklace. Something dawns on him. He stumbles off in a new direction.

HAOA'S CAVE

Day

Noro clambers down the brooding rocks, still completely distraught. Beside him, the sea crashes eternally. At the cave mouth, he cries out.

NORO
Haoa?...*Haoa?!!!*

For a moment there is no answer. Then a tiny wail reverberates from the darkness, and Haoa emerges warily from the cave with an axe in one hand. He gestures inside.

HAOA

Your daughter.

Noro stumbles in, finds Ramana lying in the dark recovering from the birth. She smiles up at him, her sight returning.

RAMANA

I hoped it was you.

Noro touches her face, overcome with love, amazement, relief, sorrow.

NORO

I thought I'd lost you.

RAMANA

I thought that's what you wanted.
(smiles)
We were both wrong.

They smother each other with affection, the baby between them, until distant shrieks float in on the wind. Haoa hovers over them protectively, axe in hand. Noro looks up, the pain returning to his face.

NORO

I know why my father left, Haoa.

HAOA

Then you're ready for this.

He moves to the canoe ramp in front of his cave and uncovers a magnificent, patched-together canoe. It's full of provisions. The prowpiece is made from the ship's sparring.

HAOA

Your wedding gift.

Noro runs his hands over the boat, looks out at the horizon where the spar points. The choice is clear. Noro turns to Haoa in gratitude.

Haoa: Mentor and Martyr

The character in *Rapa Nui* who most truly embodies the Polynesian spirit may be Haoa, the exiled canoe-builder who is Ramana's father and becomes Noro's coach for the Birdman competition. He says little and teaches by example. Through his patience, stoicism, and leadership, Noro learns not only how to survive in the race but how to hope for a future "out there," off the island.

Actor Zac Wallace found it easy to identify with Haoa. As a young man in New Zealand, he got into trouble and spent some time in jail, so was no stranger to the life of an exile. Later he became a spokesman for Maori rights and appeared in several documentaries on the Maori political activism of the early 1970s. From that experience grew a full-time acting career on New Zealand television and film. Zac also performs with his jazz band through New Zealand and Australia, where he now lives.

For Zac, the experience of working on *Rapa Nui* among people from another Polynesian culture was as important as chalking up his eighth feature film. "Polynesia is becoming more and more attractive to filmmakers," he asserts. "I think this film will show that there are Polynesian actors worthy of standing in any film, and that the story line will say to potential writers: 'Hey, there's 150, 200 years of history in Polynesia. Let's go find out what those stories are about.'

"For the people of Rapa Nui, having all these visitors from overseas living and working here may help them feel that they're not prisoners—that they too can make it off their island someday."

Above and facing page: Noro discovers Ramana and their baby safe in Haoa's cave, and they set sail for lands unknown.

NORO
Come with us.

HAOA
(shakes his head)
If I'd been braver, I'd have gone with your father...Now, if I was younger, I'd go with you.

A look passes between them. More shrieks, closer now.

HAOA
Hurry.

The patched sail is hoisted into place. Below it, Ramana sits in the boat with her child. Haoa kisses the infant's head, kisses his daughter for the last time. He joins Noro at the back of the canoe.

NORO
Which way did he sail?

Haoa points past the earth's endless curve toward the setting sun.

HAOA
Don't look back.

He and Noro push the canoe into the surf. Never looking back, Noro sets a course for the unknown. The camera speeds past him toward the horizon, and words appear on the screen:

“Archaeological evidence indicates that Pitcairn Island may have been settled from Easter Island—some 1,500 miles

Part Three

FILMMAKING AT THE ENDS OF THE EARTH

The opening sequence of Rapa Nui*...*

It is dawn. The camera rushes over ocean swells toward an island looming up in the cold gray light. As we pass over the thousand-foot cliff that plunges to the sea at Orongo, three giant stone moai *come into the frame, backlit against the rising sun. Then we float in on their empty eyes, which turn into...the sun, blinding us as it emerges from the sea.*

The figure of a young man, a messenger, races across the frame, silhouetted against the sky. We pan with him to reveal the entire mountainside covered with half-buried, monstrous statues. Then the camera moves down. Far below on the barren, rocky landscape another statue, about 33 feet high, inches toward the coast, dragged by several hundred tiny human figures, kicking up dust as it goes.

Above: On the windy clifftop near Orongo, Camera Operator Mark Spicer prepares to shoot the scene where Long Ears lower Ramana down to the Virgin Cave. Facing page: An extra in traditional body paint.

The action we've just witnessed takes less than twenty seconds on film, but took many months to get from screenplay to screen.

The director and producers scouted and chose the location.

The executive producer mapped out the logistics for supporting a film crew of several hundred on Rapa Nui over a six-month shooting schedule.

The second-unit director came to the island several months prior to actual shooting and plotted the sun's movement in the sky through the year, so that it would rise in precisely the right place in the frame for this shot.

The production manager toured the island with local and Chilean officials to guarantee the safety of archeological treasures.

The production designer devised a way to recreate the giant *moai* statues with metal frames and foam, making them light enough to maneuver but not so flimsy that they would topple in Rapa Nui's strong winds.

A hundred and fifty extras were hired, trained, placed, and directed to make the *moai* move—not on wheels but dragged over the ground on rollers, just as in ancient times.

The actor playing the messenger toughened the soles of his feet to with-

stand running at full speed over the volcanic rubble of the Orongo cliffs.

Everyone in the crew and cast prayed to the Rapa Nui gods for clear skies.... If the clouds gather, the shot is blown for the whole day.

If the gods cooperate, all these preparations come together just at the crack of dawn and the call of "Action!"

And this is only one shot out of hundreds, all but a few filmed on location in one of the most isolated spots on the planet. Shooting a major motion picture on Rapa Nui was a feat on the order of the ancient Rapa Nui culture carving and erecting their *moai*—a parallel not lost on the filmmakers. The story of how it was done is as fascinating as the tale that unfolds on the screen.

Second-unit Director Mark Illsley, who was chiefly responsible for pulling off the opening shot, remembers the making of *Rapa Nui* as a true adventure for the crew that experienced it. "It was nothing like making a film in the U.S.—more what I imagine it must have been like to make *Apocalpyse Now* or *Lawrence of Arabia.*

"When viewers see a *moai* moving across the landscape on screen, it's easy to think, 'Oh, that's just movie magic.' I just hope that what comes across on the screen is equal to what we experienced in getting it there. We really felt like we *made* this *moai*, like we moved a giant statue across this island."

Director Kevin Reynolds sits on the recumbent Monster moai *to compose a shot.*

A Five-Page Fantasy

The adventure had its genesis about 15 years ago, when director Kevin Reynolds saw a Jacques Cousteau documentary about Easter Island. Like a lot of people, he had seen pictures of the statues but knew very little else about the place. His curiosity fired—especially by the film's account of legends such as the Birdman race and the battle at Poike—Reynolds did some background reading, including Thor Heyerdahl's *Aku-Aku.* The germ of a story started to take shape in his mind, and he dashed off a five-page outline.

That was as far as *Rapa Nui* got until the summer of 1991, when Reynolds told Kevin Costner and Jim Wilson about it. His friendship with Costner dates back to 1981, when he directed the then-unknown actor in his first feature, *Fandango*, and was renewed dur-

Welcoming the Chief

Producer Kevin Costner was viewed by everyone involved in the production as its godfather—the person whose stature and influence enabled the film to be made and its crew to gather on Rapa Nui from the far corners of the world. When he and his family visited the island during the shoot, the Maori actors performed a traditional ceremony of welcome.

"It's traditional for us to greet visiting parties on our own ground with this ceremony," says Zac Wallace, "and since we are *faunoa*, or related to the Rapanui people, and had been given the key by the governor, we felt permitted to perform such a welcome here.

"When Kevin Costner visited, he was regarded as the Great Chief because he gave us all the opportunity to be here. The ceremony starts with a greeting, or *porfini*, then welcoming speeches are made and a song that enhances the speaker is usually sung by women. It is meant to warm the visitor to the land, and to the spirit of the people within the land—both those who have departed and the living who carry the weight, the joys, the loves, the sorrow of their ancestors."

Touching the guest's nose and forehead signifies "the first breath of life and the imparting of knowledge about the place they are visiting. So when we touched Kevin Costner's nose and forehead, we were saying to him, 'From us, the first breath of life, and let your ancestors mingle with mine.'"

Producer Costner and Director Reynolds confer on Rapa Nui.

ing their collaboration on *Robin Hood: Prince of Thieves*, which Reynolds directed and Costner starred in.

Meanwhile, Costner and Wilson had founded Tig Productions and gone on to make *Dances With Wolves*—thereby establishing themselves as producers who could not only bring an unusual story to the screen but attract major financial backing and studio support. All the same ingredients, and the same needs, were present in the *Rapa Nui* concept.

Jim Wilson recalls, "He walked into our office and plunked down his five-page treatment, and that was about it. We decided almost right away that we wanted to get involved." Tig was on the lookout particularly for "that little gem of a story" they could lavish care on, and this one struck an emotional chord.

Rapa Nui appealed to them partly because of its obvious affinities with *Dances With Wolves*: a historical drama of a vanished society, shot on location with a mostly indigenous cast and a message about the need to care for the land. "As producers we love the challenge of bringing exotic locations to the screen," says Wilson, "and bringing history to life." And thanks to the success of *Dances*, Costner and Wilson had the clout to finance such an unconventional project.

Of Kevin Costner, Reynolds says, "The bottom line is that he made

Rapa Nui possible because he was willing to go to bat for it. And once we were in production, he managed to keep us going without the usual interference, even though we went behind schedule and over budget."

From Screenplay to Scouting

Once Reynolds and his producers were committed, the next step was to expand the original five-page treatment into a shooting script. For this they turned to English writer Tim Rose Price, who had scripted for all realms of British film, television, and stage, including a BBC production about Captain Cook, one of the first Europeans to visit Easter Island.

Rapa Nui was the big movie challenge he had been waiting for. While Reynolds was immersed in shooting *Robin Hood*, Price traveled to the island for research that included sleeping in one of its many caves and even duplicating part of the open-ocean swim of the Birdman contest. As soon as he was free, Reynolds went to work helping to shape the script and roughing out shots.

The shooting script that emerged from this collaboration reflected their research, incorporating countless aspects of Rapa Nui's known history: from major events like the Birdman cult and toppling the *moai* to small details such as the stone "earth ovens" used for cooking. Key plot elements were drawn from island legends, such as conflict between the Long Ears and the Short Ears, and the practice of shutting women up in caves to lighten their skin. The story told on film is not an exact retelling of history—impossible in any case because there are so many gaps in the record. The filmmakers rearranged events and compressed time to create a powerful story, based on history but with plenty of fast-paced action and romance.

Late in 1991 came a decisive moment in the film's development, when Reynolds and Executive Producer Barrie Osborne visited Rapa Nui on a scouting trip. Originally this was conceived as just a fact-finding mission, a chance to get the look and feel of the place and then try to duplicate them in a more accessible location. Rapa Nui was, after all, thousands of miles from the nearest inhabited land and offered few resources to support a major film production. Electricity had come to the island a mere twenty years earlier.

Excerpt from Tim Rose Price's journal:

Slept the night alone at Orongo. Swam between Motu Iti and Motu Kau Kau. Walked the north coast to Anakena. Saw the 360° horizon from Terevaka. And I heard ancestral voices!

They dance out the night's darkness, argue the past as though it's happening now, eat for all their starved ancestors, and sing—and when they sing, Rapa Nui *is* Hiva.

This place isn't just a metaphor for the end of the world; I feel it contains the solution too—something to do with the infinite capacity of the creative imagination—refusing to be limited by horizons.

Sunset behind the lone bearded moai *at Ahu Tongariki, near Poike.*

But things didn't quite work out that way. As Reynolds relates, "When I first came here, it was just with the intent to do research—to see it firsthand and then go and make the picture somewhere else. I'd figured it was too remote; we could never do the shooting here. But after being here, seeing the quarry and Orongo and the landscape and sky...I knew I couldn't make it anywhere else."

His colleagues also came under the spell that the island casts—its incredible landscape, easygoing ways, and what Barrie Osborne calls "a *mana* that we hope will transfer itself to the film." (*Mana* is the Polynesian term for a spirit force or great presence.) They agreed that shooting on Rapa Nui was the right choice.

Laying Foundations

The immense task of assembling and equipping a film crew to shoot on location in Rapa Nui was overseen by Executive Producer Barrie Osborne, who came to the challenge well prepared. His background included Francis Coppola's *Apocalpyse Now* as well as the James Bond location epics *Moonraker* and *Octopussy*, so he was seasoned in the need to plan for every possible contingency...and then expect the unexpected. Osborne had also worked with Kevin Reynolds on *Fandango*, and had assisted since 1987 on the quest to get *Rapa Nui* filmed.

The first order of business was the delicate process of negotiating with Chilean and local officials for permission to film around the island. Because so much of Rapa Nui is archeologically and environmentally sensitive, the filmmakers had to consult with representatives from Chile's parks and forestry dept (CONAF), the Chilean Archeological and History Site Conservatory (Consejo de Monuments), as well as Rapa Nui's council of elders, governor, and mayor. They toured the island with these officials during several scouting trips, pointing out possible filming sites and arranging for clearance.

They tried to get across that this would be a very different proposition from the small documentary film crews the island was used to. Says Osborne, "When we first told the islanders we planned to make a major movie, I don't think they believed us. A lot of people have approached them with different projects, and most don't materialize. So they were

The crew sets up to shoot on the shoreline rocks of Motu Nui; a few of the more daring dived from here during lunch breaks.

skeptical that we would come back to actually make the movie."

Production Manager Zane Weiner agrees: "We knew that they had no idea of the scope and impact of what we planned. Even in this country, if you come into someone's neighborhood and tell them there will be forty trucks, and streets will be closed and stores shut down and so on, they don't really grasp it until it's happening. And this is an island that until twenty years ago wasn't even in this century. So no matter how we tried to prepare them, they couldn't know what was in store."

Another early task was to recruit a technical crew capable of such a remote and difficult location shoot. Some of the key people they called on had worked with the principals before—John Bloomfield designing costumes for Reynolds's *Robin Hood*; Production Manager Zane Weiner teaming with Osborne on other projects.

To fill other important roles they turned to the flourishing film community of Australia, because Osborne "thought it would be a good way to mount this film set in the Pacific." An August 1992 visit led them to Production Designer George Liddle, Director of Photography Steve Windon, and Stunt Coordinator Glenn Boswell, each of whom assembled a staff for his department. Certain special skills were sought; for example, grips with experience rigging cameras in impossible places (like Rapa Nui's sheer cliffs), and stuntmen with mountaineering and underwater experience.

Talking Bones

An experience Kevin Reynolds had on his first visit to Rapa Nui convinced him that there are spirits on the island, that the *mana* of the ancestors still lives in the wind. "Driving around the island, we stopped at the first *ahu* we saw, on the south coast. Walking closer, I saw the remains of a burial chamber, with some shards of bone scattered among the crumbling mossy rocks. I picked up a piece and we moved on.

"Later the same afternoon we were at a remote *ahu* on the north side, called Tepiu. It was a strange day because it was so still. The ocean was like a millpond. No wind, no crickets, just total silence. I was crawling around the *ahu*, looking underneath the burial chambers and so on, when I suddenly saw out of the corner of my eye something above me and off to the left. Then it dropped behind the edge of the *ahu*. Like it had been watching me. But when I walked around the other side, nothing was there, of course. It sent a chill up my spine, and the uneasy feeling stayed with me all day.

"That night I told our hotel owner's daughter what had happened to me—I was a little embarrassed because I don't believe in that kind of thing. When I finished she asked, 'Have you taken anything?' When I told her about the bone, she said, 'Put it back.' So I did."

In all, about 175 film people came to live and work on Rapa Nui during the six months of production. The 140 crew members and 35 actors came from every corner of the world: Australia, New Zealand, Spain, England, the United States, Canada, and Chile.

Dressing and Undressing the Cast

A big part of transporting modern-day Rapa Nui back to the seventeenth century was costuming its inhabitants who worked as extras in the film. "At first," recalls Costume Designer John Bloomfield, "they were shy about getting out of their normal clothes and going half-naked." But they soon grew into seasoned veterans, arriving on the set with clothes already off and makeup on.

Bloomfield, who had done costumes for Kevin Reynolds's *Robin Hood*, came to Rapa Nui before the start of filming to set up shop in an outbuilding of the local museum, arranging to have sewing and washing machines and other supplies shipped over from Santiago. He hired 23 islanders—people skilled in handwork and crafts—for his staff. Having also worked on film projects in Spain, he was fluent in Spanish, a great help in communicating with the local workers.

Bloomfield found little reference to use from Rapa Nui's ancient times—"most of it was destroyed." But there were enough clues to work from: the island's rock art suggested patterns, as did the tattoos seen on the *moai* and in old photos of islanders. And Bloomfield knew from other Polynesian sources how the local *tapa* cloth was made.

Tapa, the only fabric used in island garments, is made of sheets cut from paper-mulberry bark and pounded soft. The designer loved its papery look and the way it took colors. Some is still made on the island, where it is called *mahote*, but not in the quantities the film needed. "So I went to Tonga," says Bloomfield, "which has a thriving *tapa* industry and imported 3,000 square meters." The only problem with *tapa* was that it disintegrated in the rain and under hard use, so many duplicates were needed.

Other local materials used in costumes were

Left and above: Costume drawings by John Bloomfield of a competitor costumed and painted for the Birdman, and Ramana in her tapa *cloak after her time in the cave. Facing page: top left, closeup of a "Long Ear" achieved with prosthetic makeup; top right, a dancer costumed for the pre-race procession; bottom, Grandfather surrounded by Long Ear warriors in full regalia.*

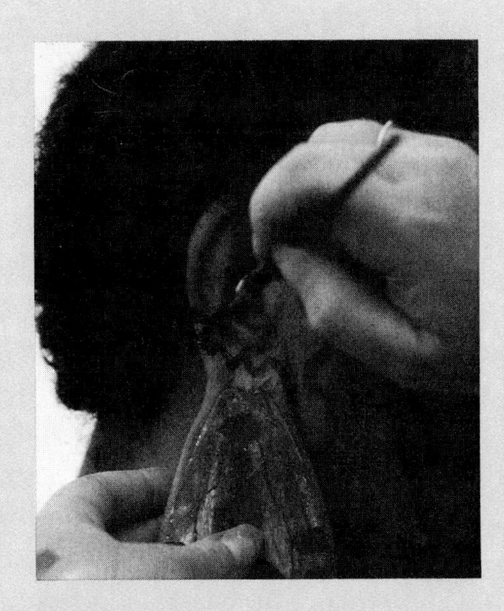

feathers, sticks, and bones. Designs for jewelry and other ornaments were borrowed from local crafts and natural inspirations. The boat-shaped hats of the Long Ear girls, worn to keep the sun off their skin, were copied from eighteenth-century engravings; these quickly became collector's items and quite a few disappeared.

"We made about 2,000 costumes in all, including the extras. It was exciting to see a big scene like the spectators at Orongo, with the extras all massed together in costumes." Regarding differences between characters, the main challenge was to distinguish between the Long Ears and Short Ears—"the Long Ears got more costuming, more decoration, like they had more of everything else."

Makeup was handled by England's Peter Frampton, who won an Academy Award for his work on *Greystoke: The Legend of Tarzan*. His experience with indigenous people in the Amazon on *The Emerald Forest* proved invaluable in designing the tattoos and body paint for *Rapa Nui*.

Ramana's overall look was a challenge, because she undergoes such a transformation after emerging from the Virgin Cave. The effect achieved with makeup and costume was "meant to look like part of the cave," says Bloomfield, "all rock colors, like some troglodyte."

Grandfather wears the brightest colors—reds, yellows, bold black designs—to reflect his importance and eccentricity.

Of Jason Scott Lee as Noro, says Bloomfield: "I don't know why they're paying me, when he's almost naked anyway. He's in such great shape that you want to cover as litle of him as possible."

After the filming wrapped, some of the costumes were left on the island for use by its local dance troupes and museum.

The filmmakers returned to Australia to complete post-production work on *Rapa Nui*, as well as some second-unit shots such as the iceberg scene—filmed off the coast of New South Wales about 50 miles north of Sydney. Among the last steps before the film's release was mixing in an innovative musical score by Stewart Copeland, formerly of the Police and renowned for his synthesis of worldwide percussion forms. So even the soundtrack of *Rapa Nui* will have an international accent.

Casting a Lost Civilization

Rapa Nui posed unique challenges for Casting Director Elisabeth Leustig. The film needed attractive, athletic young leads, strong character players for supporting roles, and a large cadre of extras. And, by the way, they must all embody a basically Polynesian type, know English for the speaking parts, and not overtax the film's budget with star salaries.

Leustig traveled around the world in search of this cast: to New York, Toronto, Australia, New Zealand, the Cook Islands, and Easter Island itself. For their leads, notes Jim Wilson, "we ended up with Sandrine Holt from Toronto, Esai Morales from the Bronx, and Jason Scott Lee from Hawaii." Many of the supporting roles were played by actors from the thriving Maori theater community of New Zealand—a gold mine for Leustig's recruiting efforts. Rapa Nui residents filled out the corps of extras.

Zac Wallace as Haoa.

Zac Wallace, a Maori now living in Australia who plays the canoe-builder Haoa, hails Leustig's efforts: "Elisabeth did me a great favor personally by casting me, because I was reunited with people from New Zealand I hadn't seen for many years. Beyond that, I think she connected with the Polynesian spirit and was able to find people who could give what the script called for. In the characters she put together, there's everything a director could want: the aggression, the madness, the stoicism."

Working with a large contingent of non-English-speaking extras and crew members was another hurdle. Even though some had a little English, it was hard to communicate the subtleties of performing a specific action or expressing an emotion. "It's not enough," says Osborne, "just to tell people, 'Your favorite is winning the race, so stand up and

The Maori Become Rapanui

Casting Director Elisabeth Leustig had the task of assembling an entire vanished population for *Rapa Nui*—not just extras, but solid, experienced actors to play important characters. The film needed actors of Polynesian ethnic type, yet since it would not be subtitled, all the speaking roles had to be filled by English speakers.

Traveling around the Pacific in search of this cast, Leustig found a motherlode in the Maori people of New Zealand, who have had an active theater community for many years. A total of 30 actors of Maori descent joined the *Rapa Nui* cast, including the major roles of Grandfather (Eru Potaka-Dewes), Tupa (George Henare), and Haoa (Zac Wallace). Although their homelands are thousands of miles apart, the actors felt a link with the Rapanui people because they share a basically Polynesian cultural history and language patterns. "There's a similar feel between the people," says George Henare, who didn't even know there *were* Polynesian people on Easter Island until two months before he came there.

Zac Wallace says, "We can hear some resemblance in the Rapanui language to our own. The terms *taina* and *toakan* for example: Here they call us the *taina*—younger brothers—and we call them the *toakan*, or elders. If they were visiting New Zealand it would be the other way around.

"Also we see some similarities in their performing arts: the dancing and chants. It's nothing new to people from Polynesia. We're born into the performing arts; it's even built into our speechmaking. And I notice that everyone here sings, or plays the guitar or ukulele, or performs in dances. It's no different from Hawaii or Tonga or Samoa ...or New Zealand."

Maori actors Gordon Hatfield (left), Cliff Curtis, and others.

cheer.'" The translator must convey and inspire the emotion the scene is meant to evoke, and be familiar enough with film vocabulary to know which actions will be effective on screen, or how to explain about actors' "marks."

Since Rapa Nui is Chilean, Spanish is the local language. With his Latino American roots and extensive film background, actor Esai Morales often stepped in to help translate for the extras, functioning almost like another assistant director during parts of the filming. The stature of his character, Make, also helped to win their attention and respect.

An Island as Sound Stage: Logistics of the Shoot

Once all personnel were accounted for, the producers could turn their attention to the massive logistical effort needed to transport them, and all their equipment and effects, to Easter Island, and then support them for the duration of filming. Comparisons to Coppola's well-known troubles in the making of *Apocalypse Now* were inevitable—and if anything, the Philippines were easier to supply than Rapa Nui.

"Zane Weiner and I made an agreement that we wouldn't draw from the resources of the island to feed our production, or take away from anything they needed for their livelihood," says Barrie Osborne. "So that meant shipping almost everything in."

"Everything" consisted of some 1,500 kilograms of food each week, and far more: clothing, medical supplies, camera equipment, even sewing and washing machines for the costumes. The production also brought in safety officers and two doctors. Back in the U.S., two medevac jets were on standby in the event of accidents or illness that couldn't be handled locally.

For transportation they were mainly dependent on the twice-weekly flights of LanChile, the only airline serving the island. Cargo space was limited and expensive, and weather conditions could play havoc with the flight schedule, so the crew sometimes went more than a week without re-supply and came close to running out of food several times. They also took advantage of the Chilean navy's offer of cargo space on an occasional ship stopping at the island, and leased an Aleutian cargo plane that flew direct from Sydney to Easter Island.

Actor Gordon Hatfield, who plays Riro, sports authentic Maori tattoos, similar to designs found on Rapa Nui.

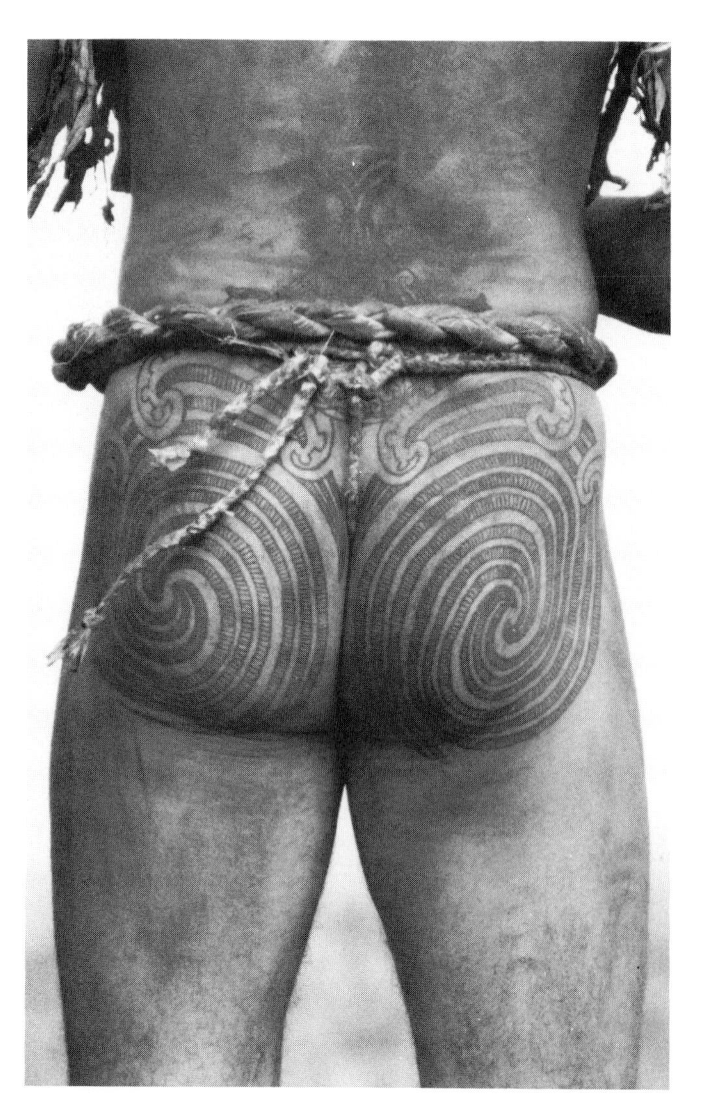

Among the chief drawbacks of limited outside contact was that the crew could not see daily rushes of film footage. By the time film was shipped out for processing and returned, "dailies" had turned into "weeklies"—and if the flight was cancelled, they might not see footage for two weeks. Not just a matter of delayed gratification, this put extra pressure on everyone to get a shot on the first take—by the time they saw the results, it was often impossible go back and redo it.

Despite the problems of being self-sustaining, the crew lived fairly comfortably on Rapa Nui. In early stages of planning, Osborne and Weiner thought they might have to live very close to the ground, a guerrilla crew with just a couple of trucks, housed in tents. "We called Outward Bound to find out how to dig toilets in the ground, purify water, and other survival techniques." As it turned out, basic comforts were more than adequate. The challenges lay elsewhere: in the island's remoteness, in the crew members' long isolation from families, in the need to tread lightly on shooting sites.

Rapa Nui's weather further tested the

"I Like to Live the Movie"

Kevin Reynolds gives direction to Jason Scott Lee.

Kevin Reynolds, whose fifteen-year dream to make a feature film about Easter Island finally came true, won universal praise from his cast and crew for his handling of the difficult location shoot on Rapa Nui.

Producer Jim Wilson calls him "one of the best 'shooters' working today: a technical craftsman who is also a writer. And I think he composes shots with the best of them."

Actor Zac Wallace says, "He knows what he want to see on the screen. He gives me clear direction but also an opportunity to apply my own method of acting. If it doesn't work he comes and talks to me quietly. He doesn't shout from behind the camera."

Best known for his deft touch with action sequences, Reynolds directed his first feature film, *Fandango*, in 1981. He conceived the idea for *Rapa Nui* at almost the same time, but stories of indigenous people were not very marketable at the time, so he put the treatment aside, moving on to direct *The Beast*, a critically acclaimed film about the Afghanistan war, and *Robin Hood: Prince of Thieves*. He also wrote several screenplays, including *Red Dawn*.

Second-unit Director Mark Illsley has worked with Reynolds on all his feature films, and appreciates that the director "likes to use a lot of second-unit material. Kevin loves all the material he can get his hands on. He can be exacting, because he knows what he wants and requires precision in getting shots as scripted. Some of the shots in this movie have been in his head for eight years, so with that kind of buildup there's extra pressure to get it right."

For Reynolds, shooting on Rapa Nui made the dream that much more real. "I like to live the movie. Part of making it was to live the adventure of coming to Easter Island and seeing what it must have been like for the characters in the film."

crew's patience and fortitude. "Being on a remote island at sea is much like being on a ship; you're subject to all the storms that pass through," Osborne notes. Winds from 40 to 70 knots were common, and it rained a fair amount. Partly cloudy skies were most common and "a cinematographer's worst nightmare," says Steve Windon, "because you can't set up dependably for a sun shot or a cloudy shot." Too, it was often colder than visitors expect of a South Pacific island, a problem mainly for actors who had to look comfortable in a loincloth and little else.

The tendency of weather conditions to change with mercurial speed was most problematic. "For example," recalls Kevin Reynolds, "you plan to shoot the village one day, but it's too windy. So you send all the extras home and move the shoot somewhere else because it's in the sun and you need sun. As soon as you get to that spot, the sun goes in and it starts raining."

Steve Windon (right) and Mark Spicer behind camera.

"It's All a Landscape Film"

Though it won't get billing on theater marquees, Easter Island itself is really the "star" of *Rapa Nui*. The filmmakers recognized instantly what a spectacular backdrop the island would make, with its pounding surf, sheer cliffs, and gaudy sunsets, for the story they planned to shoot.

To emphasize the island's sweeping scale, they chose to shoot in Cinemascope, with its anamorphic frame ratio of 2.35 to 1. (The proportion of width to height; for comparison, most films are shot at a ratio of 1.85 to 1.) Simply put, it means a wide-screen frame in which the setting will appear in all its grandeur.

Framing these memorable images was Director of Photography Steve Windon, one of the Australian film veterans recruited for *Rapa Nui*. Executive Producer Barrie Osborne had worked with Windon on a Disney picture set in New Zealand, and anticipates that his work on *Rapa Nui* will move him into the front ranks of his profession.

Like everyone on the film, Windon had problems keeping up with the island's fickle weather. "It was a challenge to match the quality of light when parts of a scene were shot separately. Unless you can shoot them in matching light, it can look like somewhere else entirely."

Windon tried to visually convey the mood shift that occurs partway through the film, with an overall change in its color tonality. "It starts in warmer tones and changes to a colder, bluer, more monochromatic look later on. This is meant to reflect the darker, more violent side of culture that's emerging."

The island's rugged terrain provided a dramatic backdrop but many hazards for the filmmakers. There are literally no paved roads on Rapa Nui, and its gentle-looking, grassy plains and slopes are in reality littered with volcanic rubble, making it a chore to hike around with equipment and dangerous for the actors who had to run across them full-tilt. Says Esai Morales, "There were times when the biggest acting challenge was not to show that it hurt."

The entire crew was tested to a rare level of physical endurance: lugging equipment up and down trails and volcanic cliffs, filming in rough seas. Fortunately cuts and bruises were the worst result.

Jim Wilson knew from the start that filming on the island would be far from easy but was surprised by the extent of logistical tangles. "Say a lens goes down, a camera goes down—you have to go all the way to Australia or Santiago.... The remoteness is the most difficult part of the production, yet it's also the charm of it. We're entirely focused here on what we're doing; there are no distractions.

"It also will give the film great power. I think when people go into the cinema and the screen comes on, the curtains go up, you will know immediately that this is like no place else on earth. I don't think it could be faked anywhere. There's something magical about this island that will come off on the screen."

Action Without "Acting"

The action centerpiece of the film is the ritual Birdman competition, where young representatives of clan chieftains engage in a sort of rough-and-ready triathlon: racing along the rim of the Orongo crater,

Christian Beazley, as the ill-fated competitor Makita, takes a stunt fall off the Orongo cliffs onto an airbag below.

climbing down a 1,000-foot cliff to the rocky beach, and swimming through heavy, shark-patrolled seas to a tiny islet a mile off the coast. There they hunt for the first egg of the migratory *manutara* bird, and race back to deliver it into the hands of their chief. The first to receive an intact egg becomes the Birdman—the island's ruler—for the coming year.

Filming climbing sequences on the cliffsides called for special camera-rigging techniques, camera operators shooting from climbing harnesses while rappeling, and extreme care on the part of the actors and stuntmen. Key grip Ray Brown was responsible for most of the cliff rigging, and cameraman Mark Spicer contributed mountaineering experience.

Mark Illsley claims that Rapa Nui offered "some of the most hazardous locations I've ever been on. Especially the Orongo cliffs, where it was a difficult 30- to 40-minute hike just to get down to the site where cameras were placed. Everything had to be backpacked down there. Then it was another 40 minutes of technical climbing to get to the beach site at the bottom of the cliff—not a location where we would normally take any film unit."

The greatest danger was not so much the cliff's steepness but its frequent rockfall. The weathered rock crumbled easily, so even secure-looking handholds and footholds had to be tested. Stunt coordinator Glenn Boswell fell once and took a watermelon-sized rock in the chest, but came to no serious harm.

Another treacherous spot was the islet of Motu Nui, where the birds

The Sunbirds Return to Rapa Nui

The Birdman cult centers on the annual migration of the *manutara* birds—sunbirds—to lay eggs on the islet of Motu Nui. Two different bird species were linked with the ritual at various times: the frigate bird and sooty tern. Frigate birds are most often depicted in the birdman petroglyphs; their great hooked beaks (the male's has a red pouch underneath) may have a sexual connotation. Though once frequent visitors, frigate birds are now extremely rare around Rapa Nui because they lay eggs only once in two years; if disturbed they won't nest at all.

Sooty terns are less impressive but more numerous. Their eggs could reliably be found each year on Motu Nui, so they became the competitors' targets. Even the terns were eventually wiped out, however; in 1983 only a single pair nested on Motu Nui.

How then were the filmmakers to depict the eagerly awaited arrival of the *manutara* birds that precedes the race? Filming wildlife is always a sensitive issue, and they wanted to handle it properly. Consulting with noted Pacific Rim ornithologist Peter Harrison, they learned of a large colony of frigate birds on Sala-y-Gómez, a windswept islet—barely more than a reef breaking the surface—partway between Easter Island and Chile.

They received permission to capture some birds temporarily, and with the assistance of Chilean wildlife experts Michel and Betsy Sallabery, Harrison and his wife Shirley Metz captured 36 frigate birds which were taken to Motu Nui aboard a chartered 112-foot yacht. There they were kept in a spacious enclosure and released a few at a time for filming. Local fishermen were commissioned to catch fish for them. "We had the best-fed frigate birds in the whole Pacific Ocean," says Harrison. The crew also scattered food in the surrounding waters to attract free-roaming birds—in all, about 150 can be seen in the shot.

None of the birds was harmed, and all were released eventually to resume their migratory lifestyle.

Ornithologist Peter Harrison holds a wild frigate bird.

nest. Heavy surge made landing (of boats or swimmers) on the rocky shore very dangerous. The swell could shift as much as 8 feet up and down, and landings had to be timed precisely. Both Barrie Osborne and Jason Scott Lee were swept off rocks and cut badly enough to require stitches.

To film sequences in the ocean, the crew had to wait for a day when the seas weren't too high. The Birdman contestants were trained in swimming the rough seas by Henri Garcia, an ex-Cousteau diver who now lives on Easter Island. For the scene where the three leaders surf back onto the beach at Orongo, some professional Australian surfers who happened to be on the island were recuited to ride the unstable reed floats.

Unique to Rapa Nui is a sporting event known as the "banana slide": hurtling down a long grassy slope on a sled made of banana trunks lashed together. Youths on the island have been doing this for as long as anyone

Mark Spicer films Esai Morales (as Make) and other competitors in the swimming sequence. For tracking shots in the water, the crew built a special "float camera" rig with a pendulum at the bottom and a counterweight 10 feet above the surface. This allowed the camera, attached to an inner tube, to stay fairly level rather than rocking wildly and causing a "seasickness" effect.

can remember. Kevin Reynolds had seen it on tape before coming to Rapa Nui, and he wanted it in the film "to show the last boyish hurrah for Noro and Make." Most of the stuntwork was done by local extras; alas, the scene had to be cut to meet the film's running time.

Lee notes that all the actors playing the Birdman competitors made a pact to look out for each other—contrary to what goes on in the story —trying to minimize the inherent hazards of the action sequences. They followed a rigorous physical regimen to prepare for them, and were blessed with a lot of luck. What they didn't need to do was "act,": the grit and strain and pain showing in their faces were for real.

Recreating a Civilization

To Production Designer George Liddle fell the task of transforming "the world's largest open-air museum" into seventeenth-century Rapa Nui. With its rugged beauty and evocative archeological sites, the island imposed its own style on the production. But the reed huts that once housed its people are gone, the islanders wear T-shirts and shorts rather than *tapa*-cloth robes like their ancestors, and the last of the great *moai* was carved hundreds of years ago. As in any historical epic, building a convincing frame for the action was critically important.

While the island's isolation made their job more difficult, the production team found an unexpected bonus: Rapa Nui is rich in people skilled with their hands, and many make their livelihood as craftsmen

One of the local Rapa Nui craftsmen at work in the Production Design shop.

and carvers of tourist goods.

"The local craftsmen have been a godsend to us," Liddle says. Up to 300 islanders were employed by the production in building the Long Ear village with its huts, walled gardens, and stone chicken houses; in making costumes; and in building the *moai*. Already adept with hand tools, they adapted with surprising speed to the use of power tools, and a number were trained in carpentry and welding. This "exchange of skills" was a benefit to both sides in the making of *Rapa Nui*.

The *moai* are the enduring symbol of Easter Island and a lynchpin of the film's plot. Some 32 of them, ranging in size from about 10 feet to 60 feet high, were constructed by Liddle's crew to meet the production's specific needs. (See the accompanying sidebar "Building *Mana* into the *Moai*.") They had to convincingly resemble the real thing (with a few centuries less age on them), yet be light and strong enough to be handled as the plot demanded. As Liddle says, it felt "like reinventing the wheel."

A sequence in which the Monster *moai* breaks loose from its moorings and slides downhill, killing a man in its path, was especially complicated to plan for. The statue had to be created in place, in a way that looked as if it had been chipped out of the surrounding rock. Then it had to slide downslope on a specially built ramp and land without being damaged, because the same statue was later mounted on a sled and transported across the island.

"We had to be careful it didn't blow over in the wind," recalls Special Effects chief Steve Courtley, "because as heavy as it was, it acted like a big kite." Wheels were installed on the *moai*, which slid on a ramp with a tracking system, winch, and brakes, at a speed of up to 16 miles per hour.

The islanders who worked on the *moai* and helped haul them across the landscape seemed to bring a special dedication to their task. "I think they felt what their ancestors must have felt," Liddle speculates. Chief Sculptor Tony Lees recalls that it took a while for the local carvers to get used to the idea that the *moai* would be destroyed after the filming. And they reacted indignantly when, after the first was created and

The Voyage of the "White Canoe"

In one of the film's climactic scenes, Hotu Matua's legendary White Canoe appears off Rapa Nui in the form of an iceberg, strayed north from Antarctic waters as occasionally happens in these latitudes. This was the only major scene not filmed on the island—the iceberg was constructed and the footage shot in Australia.

Under the direction of Production Designer George Liddle, production artist Carl Glaser erected a 40-foot-high scaffolding on a barge in Sydney Harbor. The basic shape was roughed out in chicken wire and shade cloth, then sprayed with foam and painted for a slick white surface. Then the barge was towed 50 miles up the coast to a site off New South Wales where there was no boat traffic or shoreline development to distract from the "Stone Age" setting. During filming, the berg was sprayed with water, as if melting slightly; lucite icicles and real ice were added here and there for closeups.

The scene posed a few special problems for the cinematographer, such as the need to light the actors to compensate for bright reflected light off the berg, and to carefully match the color of the water at the Australia site with the waters off Rapa Nui (the sequence uses footage from both places). The huge "Grandfather canoe" in which the Long Ears paddle out to the iceberg was used in both shots—cut into four pieces for transport to Australia.

The Australian unit films the iceberg scene.

looked too perfect, Lees "aged" it a bit by throwing rocks at it.

A Big Film on a Small Island

When a large, specialized group of outsiders descends on an isolated, relatively poor society for up to nine months, both parties are bound to be strongly affected. The makers of *Rapa Nui* suspect that the more lasting effects will be on their side.

Certainly the economic fortunes of the island rose during the filming: employment, usually only about 50 percent of the potential workforce, went up to over 90 percent during the shoot. More than 750 out of total population of 2,500 worked on the film in some capacity. This was reflected in capital gains; deposits in the local bank totaled 50 million pesos before the production arrived, and 500 million near the end of filming.

Relations with the local labor force were good with few exceptions. When problems or work stoppages threatened, each case had to be discussed individually, in a sort of town meeting approach, because there were no overall union rules. Negotiatons took place both on an individual and group level, and went on until the issue was resolved to everyone's satisfaction.

Building *Mana* into the *Moai*

"The more you look at the ancient *moai*," says Production Designer George Liddle, "the more you realize what great works of art they are, and how fantastic were the craftsmen who made them."

Liddle and his art department were charged with one of the most critical tasks in recreating ancient Rapa Nui—the construction of thirty to forty prop *moai* that convincingly resembled the original statues. Like the real statues, they varied in size and expression. They also had to be light enough to maneuver during shooting, yet sturdy enough to stand up to special-effects sequences like sliding down a hillside or being toppled from an altar platform.

The *moai* makers tried to get a head start on their task by using photos as a guide for a preliminary model, made in advance in Australia. "We were little cocky," admits Chief Sculptor Tony Lees. "I built a model from photographs I'd seen and had a computer print out the shape, ready to go.

"But when we got here and saw them in the flesh—or in the rock, so to speak—they were immensely more powerful than we'd realized. I had to go back to square one and make a model of each individual statue we planned to recreate. They're all a bit different."

The technology that Lees adapted to construct the *moai* is used in building large public sculptures and commercial sets—basically a steel frame shaped by sculptors and sprayed with polyurethane foam, which is then carved and painted to resemble stone. "It's the steel wire matrix principle," Lees explains, "a succession of hoops going in three directions, forming a 'birdcage.' That frame is covered in chicken wire and shade cloth, and finally sprayed with a few inches of foam. The result is pretty light but also rigid, easy to transport."

Much of the labor in forming and carving the *moai* was provided by local workers, who came to their task well-prepared with a long tradition of everyday carving and whittling. "Almost everyone on the island is a sculptor," Lees observes. "All the men are whittling away at little *moai* in their spare time." The language barrier posed some communication problems, overcome by the use of sign language and demonstration.

The builders tried to imbue their creations with the *mana*—the Polynesian concept of spirit force—so powerfully evident in the originals. "You could translate *mana* in different ways," says Tony Lees. "Visual strength, or maybe elegance. I like to think that at least some of ours had those qualities."

Left: Kevin Reynolds checks the ramp built for the moai *slide. Right: A 50-foot film* moai *at the Long Ear village.*

Island children working as Short Ear extras.

Employees received wages in excess of local average, as well as health and welfare benefits. The production supplied meals to all workers; donated tens of thousands of dollars in medical and other supplies to the local hospital, museum, school, and orphanage; even repainted the gymnasium. Some of the prop artifacts were donated to the local museum. The infusion of cash should help improve island's economy in general, and tourism—an important resource—is likely to increase after the film comes out.

However, Jim Wilson doubts that "we've caused any major change in life on the island. We've made a momentary impact, but I don't think a lasting one." Any rise in tourism will probably be short-lived, as it's still a very long and expensive trip to Easter Island. The filmmakers do hope that their work promotes a keener appreciation for the island's art treasures and anthropological significance. Esai Morales adds: "We want to help the island achieve its deserved renown but not lose its mystery."

Zane Weiner thinks the most profound effect may prove to be on the island's children, who were exposed to different ways of life for the first time—for many months, not just the few days most tourists stay. "They see kinds of work being done that they weren't aware of, jobs they might pursue. Some people might get interested in electrics because they worked with our electrics crew. Others might look into welding or camera arts; maybe one will be a great cinematographer some day."

Jason Scott Lee, who stayed with a local family for part of his time on the island, expresses another perspective. "It's almost as if this was still the 1600s and we were explorers arriving on a ship with an abundance of new material possessions. A lot of trading went on, curiosity about our things. But mainly I think they've lost their illusions about what goes on in a movie—kids as well as adults. Having seen what goes on behind the scenes, they now know when they're watching a stunt or special effects. I think that's healthy."

Overall, the islanders' perceptions of the filmmakers progressed from suspicion to friendliness over time. At the conclusion of shooting the producers hosted a huge *umu* (feast) for some 1,000 people, at which Barrie Osborne remembers "the feeling was of warmth and thanks all the way around." Adds Zane Weiner, "I think we've kept our promises to the people here *and* made a great film. Sometimes it's hard to do both."

For their part, the filmmakers left Rapa Nui with indelible memories of its extraordinary physical beauty and of a society that could not

Jason Scott Lee as Noro is filmed while training for the Birdman.

be more different from the film capitals of Los Angeles, Sydney, or London. Kevin Reynolds says of the experience, "You could say we've educated them in the ways of making movies, and they've educated us about being patient."

Zane Weiner was especially impressed by the closeness of the Rapa Nui community: younger people caring for the old and vice versa. "No one is not looked after here." Weiner, an avid fisherman, will also remember going out on free Sunday afternoons with diver Henri Garcia and his brother, who had a sport-fishing boat, after black marlin, tuna, mahi mahi, and other big game fish. "It's probably one of the best undiscovered places in the world to fish."

Like others, George Liddle carries a vivid picture of the island in his mind: "the sea, the sky continually changing." Barrie Osborne remembers a magical day "when we were filming at Orongo. The crater was filled with mist and right in the center appeared a full 360-degree rainbow—the first I'd ever seen." Tony Lees says simply, "Who's going to forget the time they spent in paradise?"

Ancestor Rocks

When the production needed a large source of rocks to build an *ahu* for filming, they were directed to an area where there was a large circular pile of rocks of no particular archeological significance. Still, these rocks were far from meaningless. Juan Haoa, a member of the council of elders, explained their history.

Back in the early 1900s, when the islanders were fenced into their village by sheep ranchers leasing the island, Haoa's family built this particular wall of rocks to fortify their family cave. They held out behind that wall to avoid being penned up in the village like their neighbors, and most of them died under siege there. To Haoa, at least, those rocks were precious—so the filmmakers looked elsewhere for building materials.

Safeguarding Rapa Nui's Heritage

Few places in the world are as archeologically rich as Rapa Nui, or as ecologically sensitive. The entire island is a museum—not just a dead archeological site, but a living homage to the island's past and its inhabitants. Each present-day islander finds special meaning in many parts of the landscape, known intimately as only people who live their whole lives in a very small place can. "There's so little that everything becomes very dear, very important," notes Zane Weiner. The filmmakers felt "morally as well as emotionally committed" to protect the heritage of the island, their own home for many months.

The choice of each shooting site was approved by Chilean officials, island leaders, and local experts such as archeologists Reggie Budd and Claudio Cristino. All preparations and filming were supervised by on-site representatives, who could tell the filmmakers where it was safe to

Esai Morales descends from the top of the 50-foot moai *toward the Long Ear village below.*

build on or to alter the landscape, and what places to avoid—or simply take care not to disturb buried artifacts. Archeological remains are everywhere underground, but at least 60 percent of the island has never been excavated, so no one knows exactly where new treasures might lie. And the old *moai* can sometimes be damaged just by touching. In the Rano Raraku crater, for example, the producers had to settle for their second choice of locations to film the slide of the Monster *moai*.

Inevitably some parts of the landscape and ancient sites were disturbed, so once shooting was done, Producciones Rapa Nui embarked on a restoration project. A team led by Weiner spent 8 weeks and $175,000 to restore all the areas used in filming, as well as others not touched but in need of attention. The work included road repair, replanting, and dismantling structures built for the movie, and was done mainly by local contractors under supervision of CONAF (Chile's forest service), and local authorities. Ancient *manavae* gardens were regraded, expanded, and reseeded; tour pathways improved with riprap and railroad-tie steps. A delegation from UNESCO examined and approved these efforts, which in some cases left sites in better shape than they were before filming.

The film delivers a somber message about the consequences Rapa Nui's deforestation in prehistoric times. For the palm tree grove that is gradually cut down over the course of the story, the filmmakers used mainly fake trees covered with fiberglass, or eucalyptus trunks altered to look like palms. Many of the "stumps" in the mutilated grove were just two-dimensional cutouts, convincing enough from a distance.

For the sake of realism, some 20 live trees were cut out of several hundred that remain on the island—with the knowledge and approval of CONAF—and the production arranged for all these and more to be replanted. In addition, one of the Maori actors from New Zealand, Henry Vaeoso, became interested in Rapa Nui's environmental problems and made plans with a New Zealand group to mount a tree-planting project on the island.

The metal-and-foam *moais* had to be dealt with as well. One alternative was to have them towed out to sea and burned, but this was rejected because it would release pollution. Instead, the producers arranged with the town of Hanga Roa to have them removed from Rapa Nui on a naval vessel and taken to Chile for eventual destruction as landfill. The metal frames will simply rust into the earth, and foam of this type decomposes harmlessly.

Oracle from the Sky

The Long Ear village was one of the film's key sets, and after choosing an original site, the production team found a better one—but in a more sensitive area, near the major *ahu* One Makihi. Since the set would require building, construction equipment, and burning the fake village in the climactic battle, some local officials in charge were opposed to granting permission for this site.

All the principals gathered at the site one day to review and discuss the issue. As they did so, a rare migratory bird flew over the group's heads ...and landed precisely on the spot where Kevin Reynolds wanted to build the film's *ahu*.

Mayor Alberto Hotus walked up to the bird—a species known for its shyness—and actually patted it on the head. The bird looked at him, then at the filmmakers. It took off and flew over them in a circle, landing right on the same spot. That was enough to convince the mayor and other dubious officials that the Long Ear village should be built at One Makihi.

News from the Navel of the World

Portraying a civilization that self-destructs on film—and in the very place where it happened—is bound to provoke some serious reflection on the part of the filmmakers. Jim Wilson talks about making an action-adventure movie that carries this kind of weight: "First of all, we hope people will be entertained—and then give some extra thought to film's messages: about the environment, about overpopulation, about greed. They're seeing what was once a perfect little island—not unlike our earth—that provided everything we needed to sustain a civilization, and is now in disarray.

"When I read a script, I can relate to the story better if it connects with my life in some way. I think it's significant that we all—Kevin Costner, Kevin Reynolds, myself—have families now and concerns about the world we're leaving them. The hope is that viewers will share this to some extent—that we can move the goalposts just a little."

Kevin Reynolds hopes the film succeeds in its recreation of a time and place: "Our aim is to take the audience to a place they've never been, and show them a land and people they never knew existed."

What interested Reynolds especially is how Rapa Nui can be seen as a microcosm of our world. "I think a lot of what we do on this planet—including speculating about why we're here and what might be 'out there'—are the same things these people did for more than a thousand of years in their little Navel of the World. Maybe people will realize that the earth is our 'navel of the universe,' and we have to be more aware of the consequences of our actions."

Below: Birdman figure in the procession to Orongo, just before the race. Facing page: Short Ear extras haul a 35-foot moai *toward the Long Ear village.*

Esai Morales, who plays the indomitable Make, wants the film to bring viewers a message of hope: "that we can learn from our mistakes. That even when we've cannibalized ourselves and it seems as if the world has ended, humans can go on.

"Like moving the *moai*—if we pull together, anything is possible. If, on the count of three, everybody goes in the same direction, with the same purpose, we can accomplish miracles. If only we could build a symbolic *moai* for humanity."

Warner Bros. and Majestic Films Present

A Tig Productions/Majestic Films Production
in association with RCS

A Film by Kevin Reynolds

RAPA-NUI

NORO	Jason Scott Lee
MAKE	Esai Morales
RAMANA	Sandrine Holt
HAOA	Zac Wallace
TUPA	George Henare
GRANDFATHER	Eru Potaka-Dewes

Screenplay by Tim Rose Price and Kevin Reynolds
Produced by Kevin Costner and Jim Wilson
Directed by Kevin Reynolds

EXECUTIVE PRODUCERS	Barrie M. Osborne and Guy East
CASTING BY	Elisabeth Leustig, C.S.A.
COSTUME DESIGNER	John Bloomfield
MUSIC BY	Stewart Copeland
EDITED BY	Peter Boyle
PRODUCTION DESIGNER	George Liddle
DIRECTOR OF PHOTOGRAPHY	Stephen F. Windon, A.C.S.
ART DIRECTOR	Ian Allen
UNIT PRODUCTION MANAGER	Zane Weiner
SECOND UNIT DIRECTOR	Mark Illsley
SPECIAL EFFECTS COORDINATOR	Steven Richard Courtley
STUNT COORDINATOR	Glenn Boswell

Further Reading

Paul Bahn and John Flenley
Easter Island, Earth Island
(London and New York: Thames and Hudson, Inc., 1992)

The most up-to-date, comprehensive book on Rapa Nui yet published. Bahn, an archeologist, and paleobotanist Flenley, an authority on forest ecology, have synthesized information from their own research and that of many other scholars into a readable and balanced portrait of the island's geography and cultural history, with special emphasis on the ecological catastrophe that likely precipitated the decline of its classic culture.

Steven R. Fischer, ed.
Easter Island Studies
(Oxford: Oxbow Books, 1993)

An excellent collection of articles on many aspects of the island by leading specialists.

Alan Drake
Easter Island: The Ceremonial Center of Orongo
(Woodland, Calif.: Easter Island Foundation, 1993)

A small guidebook to one of the island's prime archeological sites.

Thor Heyerdahl
Aku-Aku: The Secret of Easter Island
(Chicago, New York, San Francisco: Rand McNally and Co., 1958)

Heyerdahl's detailed and lively report on his first visit to Rapa Nui as leader of the Norwegian expedition of 1955-56. "El Señor Kon-Tiki" soon became an important figure on the island, whose inhabitants were eager to supply "artifacts" and stories to support his ideas. Despite their ill-founded aim—to prove that Rapa Nui's original settlers came from South America—Heyerdahl's explorations and experiments make fascinating reading.

Thor Heyerdahl
Easter Island: The Mystery Solved
(New York: Random House, Inc., 1989)

Heyerdahl's return visit to Rapa Nui in the 1980s produced this heavily illustrated volume, which continues his quest to show links between Easter Island and pre-Inca cultures.

Thor Heyerdahl and Edwin Ferdon, eds.
The Archeology of Easter Island
(London: Allen & Unwin, 1961)

A more scholarly treatment of the island's archeology and artifacts as investigated by the Norwegian team and others; Volume I of a larger monograph.

Georgia Lee
An Uncommon Guide to Easter Island
(Arroyo Grande, Calif.: International Resources, 1990)

The only guidebook devoted entirely to Rapa Nui; obtainable directly from the publisher. Island expert Georgia Lee has reproduced much of its rock art as drawings, and publishes the *Rapa Nui Journal* (see below).

Alfred Métraux
Ethnology of Easter Island
(Honolulu: Bishop Museum Press, Bulletin 160, 1940, reprinted 1971)

A monumental study of the island's ancient technology and customs, by an ethnographer and one of the leaders of the Franco-Belgian expedition of 1934-35. His colleague, archeologist Henri Lavachery, did groundbreaking work on Rapa Nui's rock art.

Alfred Métraux
Easter Island
(London: André Deutsch, 1957)

A more general, popular exposition of Métraux's studies.

Katherine Routledge
The Mystery of Easter Island
(London: Sifton, Praed & Co., 1919)

The courageous and pioneering Englishwoman Mrs. Katherine Scoresby Routledge spent 17 months on Rapa Nui during the World War I years, conducting archeological surveys, taking photographs, and recording the islanders' memories and traditional stories. An invaluable source of information about the island.

David Stanley
South Pacific Handbook
(Chico, Calif.: Moon Publications, 5th edition, 1993)

Stanley's excellent regional guide contains a 10-page section on Easter Island with generally reliable information.

Paul Theroux
The Happy Isles of Oceania: Paddling the Pacific
(New York: Random House, Inc., 1991)

During his sojourn in the South Pacific, travel writer Theroux spent a few weeks camping and kayaking around Rapa Nui, which he describes in his usual trenchant style.

Rapa Nui Journal
Georgia Lee, editor and publisher
(P.O. Box 6774, Los Osos, CA 93412)

A lively quarterly journal of news and notes from Easter Island, reports on scholarly progress and new publications, and other information.

About the Authors

Kevin Reynolds

In 1983 Kevin Reynolds directed his first feature film, *Fandango*, for Steven Spielberg's Amblin Productions. In the lead role he cast a relatively unknown actor named Kevin Costner, and a lifelong friendship between the two was born. They joined forces again in 1990 when Reynolds directed Costner in the Warner Bros. hit *Robin Hood: Prince of Thieves*, and shortly thereafter Costner's Tig Productions took on the development of Reynolds's treatment for *Rapa Nui*. Reynolds's other directing assignments include the critically acclaimed film *The Beast*, about the war in Afghanistan, and he has written several original screenplays including *Red Dawn*.

Tim Rose Price

English writer Tim Rose Price has scripted material for all realms of film, television, and stage. His credits include *A Dangerous Man: Lawrence After Arabia*, produced by David Puttnam and winner of the International Emmy and the Grand Award at the New York Festival, and the critically acclaimed *Rabbit Pie Day* and *Border* for the BBC. He is currently producing his own film, *The Serpent's Kiss*, with RPB and Miramax, but it was his unproduced screenplay, *Pointing Bones*, that brought him in touch with Kevin Reynolds and led to their collaboration on *Rapa Nui*, for which Price traveled to the island to do first-hand research.

Ben Glass

An actor turned photographer, Ben Glass brought an extensive background in theater arts to his early work in commercial photography and publicity portraits. His first assignment shooting stills for a major feature was Tig Productions's *Dances With Wolves*, and those images also appeared in an illustrated book about the landmark film. Glass has since done location still photography for *Young Guns II*, *My Cousin Vinnie*, *The Bodyguard*, and *Wyatt Earp*. After that shoot he took some time to fulfill a long-term ambition: his first directing project.

Acknowledgments

Illustration Sources

All photographs are by Ben Glass unless otherwise identified below. Books from which multiple illustrations were reprinted are identified as follows: *Easter Island, Earth Island* (Paul Bahn and John Flenley) as *EIEI*; and *Easter Island: The Mystery Solved* (Thor Heyerdahl) as *EITMS*.

Page

10 Map, Annick Petersen, *EIEI*.
10 Drawing, Georgia Lee, *EIEI*.
14 Map, after Sebastian Englert, *EIEI*.
15 Engraving, Duché de Vancy, 1786, *EIEI*.
17 Engraving, William Hodges, 1774, *EITMS*.
20 Drawing, Sydney Parkinson, 1769, British Museum.
22 Drawings, left: Stephen Molnar, from E. Bacon (ed.), *Vanished Civilizations*, 1963; center and right: Y. H. Sinoto, from P. Bellwood, *The Polynesians*, 1987.
24 Engraving, William Hodges, 1786, *EIEI*.
28 Drawing, Georgia Lee, *EIEI*.
30 Drawings, Georgia Lee, *EIEI*.
33 Drawing, from T. Heyerdahl and E. Ferdon (eds.), *Archeology of Easter Island*, 1961.
34 Photo, Georgia Lee, *EIEI*.
34 Drawing, Stephen Molnar, *Vanished Civilizations*.
36 Drawings of *umu pae*, R. Förster, *Guia de Campo Arqueologica*, 1986.
38 Drawings of *ahu*, M. Bernizet, 1786, *EITMS*.
41 Drawing, Annick Petersen, after Chica, from *A la découverte de l'île de Pâques*, 1985.
42 Drawing, from Jean-Pierre Adam, *Le Passé Recomposé*, 1988.
45 *Kavakava* figure, *EITMS*.
46 Drawings by William Mulloy, from T. Heyerdahl and E. Ferdon (eds.), *Archeology of Easter Island*, 1961.
46 Photo, Georgia Lee, *EIEI*.
47 Photo, Mark Oliver, *EIEI*.
50 Drawing, Georgia Lee, *EIEI*.
51 Drawing, *rongorongo* glyphs, from T. Heyerdahl, *Aku-Aku: The Secret of Easter Island*, 1958.
115 Photo, Nigel Malone, Tig Productions.
122 Photo, Leo Pakarati, Tig Productions.
147 Photo, Nigel Malone, Tig Productions.

We are grateful to the following for permission to reprint copyrighted material:

Allen & Unwin: from *Archeology of Easter Island*, Vol. 1 of *Reports of the Norwegian Archeological Expedition to Easter Island and the East Pacific*, T. Heyerdahl and E. Ferdon, eds., 1961.
Bra Böcker: from *Easter Island: The Mystery Solved*, by Thor Heyerdahl, © 1989 by Thor Heyerdahl.
The British Museum.
Editions du Seuil: from *Le Passé Recomposé*, by Jean-Pierre Adam, 1988.
Georgia Lee.
Mark Oliver.
Rand McNally & Company: from *Aku-Aku: The Secret of Easter Island*,by Thor Heyerdahl, © 1958 by Thor Heyerdahl.
Republic of Chile, CONAF (Corporacíon Nacional Forestal): from *Guia de Campo Arqueologica*, 1986.
Thames and Hudson, Ltd.: from *Easter Island, Earth Island*, by Paul Bahn and John Flenley, © 1992 Thames and Hudson, Ltd., London; text © 1992 Paul Bahn and John Flenley; from *The Polynesians*, by P. Bellwood, 1987; and from *Vanished Civilizations*, E. Bacon, ed., 1963.

Special Thanks

The publisher and editor wish to thank the following for their special contributions to this book:

From Thames and Hudson, Ltd., London: Jamie Camplin, Ian Middleton, and Colin Ridler, for arranging permission for us to reprint generous amounts of material from the definitive book *Easter Island, Earth Island*.

Paul Bahn, co-author of *Easter Island, Earth Island*, who kindly reviewed and commented on portions of the manuscript for this book, and Georgia Lee, who provided information about Rapa Nui as well as illustrations.

Executive Producer Barrie M. Osborne, who supplied extensive background information on the production and reviewed parts of the manuscript. Also from Producciones Rapa Nui, Production Manager Zane Weiner, who shared his stories and snapshots, and Kathleen Switzer, assistant to Kevin Reynolds.

From Tig Productions: Ed Gorsuch, who conducted the interviews on which the production story and cast profiles are partly based; Lynne Whiteford, whose efficient and cheerful assistance throughout the project was truly indispensable; Allison Conant; Moira McLaughlin; Kathleen McLaughlin; and Magaly Doty.

From Majestic Films : Guy East and Tristan Whalley.

Rob Friedman, Dawn McElwaine, Mary Murphy, Diane Sponsler, and Michael Harkavy of Warner Bros.

The staffs of Walking Stick Press and Newmarket Press, especially Linda Herman, Miriam Lewis, Keith Hollaman, Joe Gannon, and Grace Farrell.

Photographer Ben Glass, whose images evoke the mystery of ancient Rapa Nui and its amazing culture and who helped with picture captions; and his photographic assistant, Leo Pakarati.

Above all, we thank Kevin Reynolds, Tim Rose Price, and producers Kevin Costner and Jim Wilson for their individual contributions to this book, and for the combined inspiration, talent, and perseverance that brought *Rapa Nui* to the screen.